Italian parsley
Madagascar vanilla pods
mint
nutmeg
oregano
panch phoran
smoked Spanish paprika
pasilla de Oaxaca chili
tonka beans
rosebuds
star anise
thyme
West Indian bay leaf
turmeric

Seasoned

Recipes *and* Essays *from* The Spiceman,

Costas Halavrezos

For Jeff –
May your cooking and
your life always be
well-spiced!
All the best,
Costas
2014

NIMBUS
PUBLISHING

Nimbus Publishing Limited
3731 Mackintosh St, Halifax, NS B3K 5A5
(902) 455-4286 nimbus.ca

Printed and bound in Canada
NB1106

Design: Peggy Issenman, Peggy & Co.
Illustrations: Joanna Close
Cover photos: Mike Tompkins

Library and Archives Canada Cataloguing in Publication

Halavrezos, Costas, author
Seasoned : recipe and essays from the spiceman / Costas Halavrezos.

Issued in print and electronic formats.
ISBN 978-1-77108-080-4 (bound).—ISBN 978-1-77108-081-1 (pdf).
—ISBN 978-1-77108-083-5 (mobi).—ISBN 978-1-77108-082-8 (epub)

1. Spices. 2. Cooking (Spices). 3. Cookbooks. I. Title.

TX406.H34 2013 641.3'383 C2013-903439-0
C2013-903440-4

Canada

Canada Council for the Arts Conseil des arts du Canada

NOVA SCOTIA Communities, Culture and Heritage

Nimbus Publishing acknowledges the financial support for its publishing activities from the Government of Canada through the Canada Book Fund (CBF) and the Canada Council for the Arts, and from the Province of Nova Scotia through the Department of Communities, Culture and Heritage.

To my essential ingredients:

Jennifer and the Three Super Siblings:

Nick, Al, and Maria

Contents

Preface

A World of Difference

It's made a world of difference! I love it when customers say that after cooking with my spices. It means they've discovered that the best complement to top-quality local produce, meat, and seafood is top-quality spices.

Spices add pleasure to everyday life, and who couldn't use more of that? The pleasurable experience can start in your kitchen, with the aroma of ingredients seasoned with cumin, cardamom, and allspice. The scents will greet your guests at the door, guiding them to the visual treat of a sauce rich in hues of saffron or turmeric. The pleasure continues as you taste a delicious, well-spiced meal that inspires good conversation and contentment. No matter how modest the meal, spices elevate it.

The "world of difference" endorsement is a reward in itself. It affirms the decision I made in 2010, when I retired from CBC Radio and took a chance on what might seem to be an eccentric switch: from seasoned journalist to neophyte spice merchant. The endorsement could also be literally rewarding: it might mean that I now have a new repeat customer.

"World of difference" generally describes a positive change. Someone shows you an easier way to do a previously frustrating task, and *presto!* frustration disappears. With spices, it can mean that after your first taste of freshly ground "00000 Grade" cinnamon from the Sri Lankan community of Cinnamon you'll never gain buy bulk ground cinnamon (often mixed with its coarser cousin, cassia).

But if "a world of difference" connotes desirable change, how is it that differences, wherever they exist in the world, can fuel distrust, hate, and violence? That was the case in every serious story I covered for more than thirty years as a CBC Radio journalist, most of the time as a host/interviewer. We are often exhorted to "celebrate difference," but the sad fact is that perceived difference is at the root of every conflict. Differences in belief system, cultural background, financial resources, personal taste, language, political loyalty, class, religion, race, gender, or power can generate enough friction to create smoke and, occasionally, fire.

While I'm retired from the world of journalism, I still consume news from many sources. I'm still intrigued with the question of how a journalist should best deal with the people who embody the differences at the heart of a story. It's easy to hide behind the role of devil's advocate in order to pose inflammatory or provocative questions, especially to a person in an unsympathetic—or worse, emotionally vulnerable—position. This has always struck me as a sign of arrested development in an interviewer and intellectual dishonesty in a news organization. On the other hand, an interviewer has a duty to his audience to dismantle illogical statements and ask uncomfortable questions, to point out missing threads in elegant tapestries of spin. Politely, of course, it's more delicious that way.

Someone once quipped, *Anyone who thinks he knows everything needs to be told a thing or two*. Whether it's in the Middle East, the House of Commons, or a sports bar, nothing is more boring than a person who believes his or her position is unassailable and non-negotiable, and that anyone who sees things differently just doesn't "get it."

As a journalist, I had to fight a normal human reaction. I had to develop enough detachment to listen carefully to arguments that didn't remotely reflect my understanding of a situation, to arguments that pressed the buttons of my preconceptions or ignorance. But that detachment allowed me to ask more critical questions of someone whose point of view I might naturally tend to favour (always a challenge in David vs. Goliath stories).

One of the unforeseen consequences of working to appreciate these opposing arguments was that over time, I felt my supply of personal opinions trickling away. Rather than trying to adjudicate and (privately) choose a winner, I became more interested in discovering whether I could find any common ground between parties who personified the "differences" in question. Finding common ground, even a small patch of it, suggested the potential for movement. And whether it's in fiction or in life, a narrative of movement is more compelling to me than one of intransigence.

I was always in the public broadcasting game for the long haul, and that meant it was essential for me to cultivate a reputation as a fair and honest broker, rather than as an advocate or crusader. As an extension of that unsexy, rather dispassionate approach, I also felt I had to make a bargain with myself: I would eliminate, as much as possible, any details of my personal life while on-air. Why? Well, for several reasons. Being able to turn on a microphone and speak to tens of thousands of people every day is a rare privilege. That's already more than a fair share of public exposure for one person. As a host with a public broadcaster, I had to deliver the work of colleagues who researched, wrote, and technically contributed to the show without ever being heard. I had to make guests comfortable on what might be the only day in their lives they'd speak to that large an audience. There was already enough of me every day. There had to be ample room for all those others.

But people also infer the strangest things from self-revelation on the radio. On a trivial level, mention that you have a cat and dog people will dismiss you as "one of those crazy cat twerps." More seriously, consider a host interviewing a couple that has been unable to conceive, after years of emotional stress due to heroic but failed medical efforts. If the host has been in the habit of using the airwaves to share every cutesy comment and document every developmental stage of his children, the couple might assume (incorrectly) that the interviewer couldn't possibly appreciate their pain.

Conversely, I found that in the absence of personal information, people attributed all kinds of good qualities to me that I didn't deserve. And to the most generous (imaginative? deluded?) radio listeners, I must make full disclosure: I am not tall and handsome. Sorry about that, but I think you'll get over it.

As my career in public broadcasting recedes further in the rear-view mirror every day, one of the main contrasts you'll find is that this collection of essays is laced with personal information: family, friends, where I live, where I eat and drink, preferences in music, pet peeves—you name it. The lid's off. Since I'm no longer bound by the bargain to keep my private life out of the discussion, I now feel free to even (*gasp!*) express my opinions.

These essays began as part of the weekly newsletter I send to customers who subscribe to it at my table in the Historic Farmers' Market in the old Alexander Keith's Brewery in Halifax. I didn't need to start writing a newsletter, but perhaps after decades of writing to daily deadlines in radio, I was sucked into a writing vacuum. Perhaps I'd bitten my tongue too many times. So every Friday, I compose a newsletter that might describe the ingredients in a spice blend I'm introducing the next day, or tell customers about the new Madagascar vanilla pods I'll have available…right after I write a few hundred words on events or people or phenomena whose connections I've been trying to work out.

Fittingly, I recently stumbled on an article by Christy Wampole, who points out that the Italian word for "essay," *saggio*, is derived from *assaggiare*, to sample, taste, or nibble food. So recipes are perfect partners for personal essays. My newsletter always includes one or two, which makes it easier to contemplate using Lebanese Seven Spice, Ethiopian Berberé, or a smoky Mexican Tlaleloco Rub for the first time. I'm including several kitchen-tested favourites, mainly one-pagers that could make a world of difference in your enjoyment of home cooking.

While I used to seek common ground between opposed interviewees, these days, I try to find it with the curious customer who claims to like good food but says, *I never cook with spices*. I invite them to sniff a sample of Tajine Spices or Creole Blend or Sri Lankan Black Curry. I then ask what they like to cook (vegetarian? poultry? BBQ?) and show them a recipe that uses their favourite ingredients, but with spices. I try to create movement towards the deliciously different world those spices reveal.

I hope you'll be as indulgent as my customers, who've tolerated my rambling prose every Friday for the past few years.

I

Do You Hear What She Heard?

Put yourself in someone else's shoes for a minute and tell me how you'd react in the following situation. To be precise, the shoes are the high heels of a hair stylist with electric-tangerine hair and symmetrical tattoos that sweep up out of her camisole over her collarbones and up both sides of her neck to points below her earlobes. A grandfatherly sort in a plaid flannel shirt and jeans has just settled into her chair at the mall salon. She notes that his hair length is about four to six weeks past its Best Before Date. Perhaps the young stylist is musing that it's a shame how some older people seem to start losing interest in their appearance. As she's about to cover him with the black plastic cape, his cellphone rings. He asks her permission to take the call. She says sure. Then she hears half of a conversation.

Hello.
Oh, hi. What's up?
Yeah, I heard there were problems with the, uh, supply. What else do you have?
From where?
Interesting.... Good stuff?
No. If you say it's good, I trust you. How much?
Same price as the other stuff?
Fine. I'll take a kilo.

I notice the stylist's eyes widening in the salon mirror. What does she think she is hearing? Is grandpa a drug dealer? The mild-mannered mastermind of a ruthless international cocaine cartel? Will law enforcement dudes in black come busting in with guns drawn at any minute?

Nothing so dramatic. But there was an international subtext to that cryptic half-conversation. I was simply taking a call from Eric, the sales manager of Spice Trekkers/Épices de Cru—my suppliers in Montréal. He was telling me that he couldn't fill this week's order for vanilla pods from Papua New Guinea.

"PNG," as it's known, had had a very poor year, causing problems with both the quality and reliability of its vanilla exports. But Madagascar's production of high-quality vanilla was still strong, and the price was the same as the PNG. So I ordered some, because so many of my customers had started buying the aromatic, sticky pods to flavour desserts (custards, crème caramel, ice cream) and to make their own Vanilla Extract or Vanilla Sugar (see p. 9).

When the spice shipment arrived three days later, I immediately opened the bag of vanilla. The pods curve at one end like a shepherd's crook and are about six inches long (slightly longer than PNG pods). They have a rich, complex aroma—especially when you open a bag that contains a kilo of them.

For you botanists, the PNG vanilla is *V. tahitiensis,* but Madagascar grows *V. planifolia* (or *V. fragrans),* whose origins can be traced to Central America, where it was first cultivated by the Mayans. The variety I purchased is most

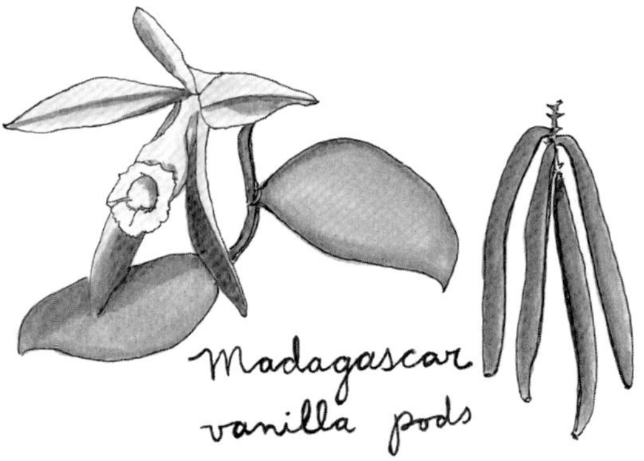

commonly known as Bourbon vanilla. And no, that has nothing to do with the modern booze. It takes its name from Île Bourbon, a former French colony, now called Île de la Réunion. That was just one of the places where *V. planifolia* was transplanted—from the Caribbean to Uganda and the Philippines.

Vanilla comes from an orchid vine (with a rather plain-looking flower), and its preparation is labour-intensive, taking from six to nine months. The reason we're able to enjoy it is one of the more remarkable stories in the history of spices. It has to do with a twelve-year-old nineteenth-century slave named Edmond Albius, who discovered how to hand-pollinate the vanilla orchid. And his discovery meant that vanilla could be cultivated in any part of the world where climate would allow.

The story of Albius is fascinating, but bittersweet. When slavery was outlawed, he found a job in a kitchen but was convicted of stealing jewelry. He served half of a ten-year sentence before being released in recognition of what he had done for the vanilla industry. Not to put too fine a point on it, but I suspect the profits enjoyed by plantation owners on Réunion—thanks to his discovery—far exceeded the value of what Albius had been convicted of stealing. He died in poverty at the age of fifty-one.

The day after the delivery, I sent out my free weekly spice e-newsletter and offered my three remaining PNG vanilla pods to the first person at Halifax's Historic Farmers' Market to compliment me on my new haircut. The pods were gone by 7:15 A.M.

And by the way, what I'm peddling is perfectly legal. But my hair stylist still doesn't know for sure.

Information on Vanilla Pods

Vanilla pods (or vanilla beans) are the fruit of orchid plants grown mainly in Madagascar (three-fourths of world supply), Mexico, Tahiti, Réunion, New Caledonia, Mauritius, Comoro, Indonesia, Uganda, Tongo, and Papua New Guinea. The bean pods are harvested before fully ripe, then soaked in hot water, rolled in blankets to "sweat," dried in the sun, and slowly fermented. The resulting dark brown pod yields about a ½ teaspoon of seeds. (A recipe for four to five people uses about a quarter teaspoon of seeds.) Although traditionally used in desserts, vanilla can also be used, sparingly, to season poultry, fish, or seafood dishes.

Storage

Store your vanilla pods in a glass bottle and keep in a cool, dark place. Do not refrigerate or freeze. If you see a white, crystalline substance on the pods, that's all right—it's probably just *vanillin*, the active ingredient. If you're not using the pods, it's actually recommended that you open the bottle and let air circulate every month or two.

Working with Vanilla Pods

Method 1

1. Open vanilla pod by gently cutting a shallow slit lengthwise. Try not to cut all the way through.
2. Extract the tiny black seeds by scraping inside the pod with a small knife or spoon.
3. Add about ¼ teaspoon of seeds directly to recipe.

Method 2

1. Steep the vanilla pod in hot liquid, such as milk or cream.
2. Add the liquid to the preparation (such as custard or crème brûlée).
3. Thoroughly rinse the pod and put it back in the cupboard, dry.
4. Vanilla pod can be used a second time. After that, use the seeds to season a third recipe.

Method 3: Vanilla Extract

1. Store vanilla pods in a glass jar with a tight-fitting lid. Fill it with 40 per cent-proof vodka or rum.
2. When you need vanilla seeds, remove a soaked pod from the jar, clip off the bottom end, and squeeze out as many seeds and as much juice as you need. Replace the pod in the jar for the next use.
3. When the pod no longer has seeds, keep in the same jar (or new jar full of vodka/rum) to create top-quality Vanilla Extract.
4. In 2–3 months, Vanilla Extract will be well-flavoured and will keep indefinitely.

Method 4: Vanilla Sugar

Vanilla sugar is used in many European dessert recipes.

1. Mix 3 vanilla pods (or the scraped-out seeds from 1 vanilla pod) with 2 cups sugar in a glass jar with an airtight lid.
2. Every few days, shake it up.
3. In 1–2 weeks, sugar will be flavoured and ready for use.

Clafoutis

Vanilla Beans

SERVES 8

Clafoutis (*cla-FOO-tee*) is a traditional, custardy and fruit-studded French dessert with as many variations as there are farm kitchens in France. This one comes from cookbook author Susan Herrmann Loomis, who learned it while living in rural Normandy. It was then tweaked by Louise Renault of CBC Radio's *Information Morning* in Halifax. The vanilla is used as in Method 2 (see p. 9). While classic clafoutis features cherries, use any fresh seasonal fruit you like.

1½–2 cups diced rhubarb (or cherries, strawberries, blueberries, raspberries)
½ of 1 vanilla bean
1 cup milk
½ cup heavy (35%) cream
3 large eggs
½ cup sugar
½ cup all-purpose flour
⅛ teaspoon salt
½ teaspoon almond extract *or* 2 tablespoons rum

1. Preheat oven to 400°F (200°C).
2. Butter and lightly flour a 9 × 2-inch-deep baking dish (non-reactive). Add a layer of chosen fruit.
3. Split the ½ vanilla bean and scrape seeds into a saucepan; add bean pod. Add milk and cream.
4. Heat at medium-high until small bubbles begin to rise.
5. Remove from heat. Beat eggs in medium bowl until thick and pale, while slowly adding sugar.

6 Sift flour and salt together and add to egg mixture in four stages, beating slowly and mixing well after each addition.

7 Remove vanilla bean from milk. Rinse, allow to dry, and use to make Vanilla Sugar (see p. 9).

8 Slowly drizzle milk into egg-and-flour mixture, beating slowly. Add almond extract or rum and combine.

9 Pour batter on top of fruit.

10 Bake Clafoutis in middle of oven for 30 to 40 minutes, until puffy, browned, and set in the centre.

11 Serve warm or at room temperature.

Lemon Vanilla Syrup

Vanilla Beans

MAKES 4 CUPS

2 cups fresh-squeezed lemon juice
2 cups water
2¼ pounds sugar
2 vanilla beans

1 Mix lemon juice, water, and sugar in a large pot.

2 Slit open vanilla pods and scrape out seeds, then add seeds and scraped pods to pot.

3 Bring to a boil and leave for 5 minutes.

4 Allow to cool. Place in a bottle. Should keep in the refrigerator for 1 month.

❧ 2 ❧

Keats, the Harvest Season, and Varmints

Season of mists and mellow fruitfulness,
Close bosom-friend of the maturing sun;
Conspiring with him how to load and bless
With fruit the vines that round the thatch-eves run…
–From "To Autumn" by John Keats (1795–1821)

If there were a poet laureate of farmers' markets, it would be John Keats. It's impossible to watch my fellow vendors stock their tables with freshly picked apples, squashes, pears, carrots, kale, and cabbage early on a September morning without recalling the mood evoked by "To Autumn."

To bend with apples the moss'd cottage trees,
And fill all fruit with ripeness to the core;
To swell the gourd, and plump the hazel shells
With a sweet kernel…

I first read "To Autumn" as a teenager inside the brick-and-cinder-block walls of St. Malachy's Memorial High—a beloved inner-city Saint John school surrounded by concrete sidewalks and asphalt streets. But the poem's melodious lines always transported me to the rolling, furrowed fields, pastures dotted with tall daisies and buttercups, and short, gnarled apple trees on my maternal grandparents' farm in Barnaby River, New Brunswick. And now, every September and October, the bounty of the harvest always makes me think of Keats.

But lately, a terrible thought has occurred: the biggest contemporary fans of Keats are obviously raccoons and starlings. This morning, I went out on the deck to see the latest overnight damage in the *season of mists and mellow fruitfulness*. Most of the deck is shaded by grapevines, which are supported by a sturdy pergola. It's as close as I can get to Greece in the Maritimes. In a fantasy life (which continues to elude me), I'm out there right now with my feet propped up, reading a book and sipping cool, freshly pressed apple cider. Keats had something to say about that autumnal product, too: *by a cyder-press, with patient look, Thou watchest the last oozings hours by hours.*

But in my actual life, I'm sitting indoors at the computer, still fuming about:
(a) the flower pot—glazed by the late Sue Klabunde and knocked over last night (but thankfully, not broken)—with its ripe Portuguese peppers and potting soil spewed over the deck;
(b) the smeared islands of grape skins and pits;
(c) the large, fresh coil of raccoon scat.

I assume the last insult was deposited only because raccoons can't yet march into a hardware store and buy tins of spray paint to tag the sites of their raids.

Furthermore, I had the uncomfortable feeling that the fat, furred marauders were now resting nearby in a cool, hollow tree trunk (*sound asleep, Drows'd with the fume of poppies*). Then, at dusk, they'll turn again to Keats to fire up for another invasion, reflecting on the poet's mouth-watering description of ripe fruit and berries (*Summer has o'er-brimm'd their clammy cells...*). And after they've worked themselves into a poetry-fuelled frenzy, they'll set out to gorge themselves on whatever we've dared to nurture all summer.

I suspect some of you might consider it a moral failing that I don't look upon these messy harvests by our wild friends as a fair tax to pay for inhabiting their stomping grounds. Tough. I can live with the bad rep. Today, all I can think of is "live trap." On a more serious note, I witnessed the disaster raccoons can wreak on a commercial vineyard when I helped with a harvest in Debert a few years ago. The night before, raccoons had found the one section of fencing that wasn't electrified, climbed through, ripped the plastic bird-mesh, and trashed more than half the year's crop. Then starlings arrived at dawn to swarm through the breach and plunder what was left. The one-two punch wiped out any possible profit from an entire year's work.

In the meantime, I'll seek consolation for my relatively small losses in the sure bet that Saturday's market will yield happier signs of the season: Tables groaning with fresh produce, aisles filled with the bustle of shoppers and the tunes of buskers, lines from Keats floating through my mind. And not a raccoon in sight.

Spiced Pear Clafoutis

Gingerbread Spice

SERVES 8

My market table is just a few paces away from Boates Farm's array of organic apples, pears, ciders, and vinegars. I'm especially fond of the father-and-son team's Bosc pears. The leathery-looking but thin skin of the Bosc covers a firm, sweet flesh that's much easier to slice for this classic dish than other, juicier varieties, but any pear will do. The slices absorb Gingerbread Spice (ginger, allspice, cinnamon, mace, and anise) beautifully, and float half-submerged in their sweet batter as they bake to a golden hue.

Now, I know purists will insist that a true clafoutis can only contain cherries—with pits. This recipe is, technically, something called a *flaugnarde.* Call it what you like, it's delicious. It also works well with apples. And please, bake this in an 8 × 12-inch pan. If you pour the batter into an 8 × 8-inch pan, you'll end up with a bizarre thing that looks like a square castle with four turrets. Don't ask me how I know this.

¼ cup raisins *or* currants
2 tablespoons rum *or* sherry
4 pears
2 teaspoons ground Gingerbread Spice, divided
6 tablespoons honey *or* maple syrup, divided
4 eggs; 2 egg yolks
½ cup sugar
4 tablespoons melted butter
7 ounces milk
3 tablespoons heavy (35%) cream
1 cup all-purpose unbleached flour, sifted

1. Soak raisins or currants in rum or sherry. Let rest for ½ hour.
2. Peel, core, and cut pears into slices.
3. Sprinkle pear slices with ½ the Gingerbread Spice and ½ the honey or maple syrup. Mix well and let soak.
4. Heat oven to 425°F (220°C).
5. Place eggs and yolks in a bowl with sugar, melted butter, and remaining spice. Mix well.
6. Add milk, cream, and liquid from pears. Mix well. Reserve pear slices.
7. Add flour to liquid ingredients and mix gently. Add raisins or currants and their liquid.
8. Butter and lightly flour an 8 × 12-inch cake pan. Pour mixture into pan.
9. Spread pear slices evenly over batter.
10. Bake in oven, 25–30 minutes, until clafoutis puffs up and fruit is cooked.
11. Remove from oven and top with remaining honey or maple syrup.
12. Serve warm or at room temperature.

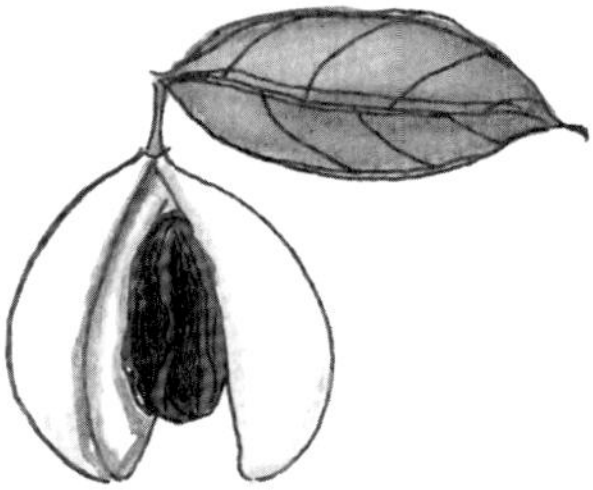

mace

3

Recipe Dread

Would you like to hear my recipe?

Those seven deceptively innocent words used to make me break out in a cold sweat during those long-ago days when I hosted the phone-in on CBC Radio's *Maritime Noon*. The well-meaning question was always guaranteed to make both our technician and director look up from their work (twiddling knobs to prevent feedback and phone-line hum; writing down the names of callers and their communities) with looks of evil glee.

It was Squirm Time for the host.

Well, I'd start, *that's all right...the way you described the aroma of that Chocolate Mackerel Banana Loaf baking in your grandmother's wood stove was just delightful.*

Oh, it's really simple, the caller would respond, oblivious to the subtext. *It'll only take a few seconds!*

At this point, the technician would lean back, knowing that all of us—including the listeners—were in for a ride that would take more than a few seconds. The director would be slapping the desk in wicked anticipation.

Well, heh, heh—we have several callers on the line... I'd counter. This was true. I hoped it would imply that since we weren't soliciting recipes on today's show (or ever), it would be insensitive to steal airtime from callers waiting to address the actual topic.

First of all, the caller would forge on, ignoring the rising tone of distress in my voice, *not any chocolate will do.*

It's not that I doubted the great affection the caller held for a recipe handed down for generations on a yellowing piece of foolscap, spattered with tea and grease and now missing essential elements (*I forget whether it was two or four mashed mackerel fillets—that part of the recipe got torn off ages ago. But you have to make sure all the bones have been removed. Now the best way to do that…*).

It wasn't the potential chemical disasters, either (*Are you sure about mixing the vinegar and baking soda with the yeast?*).

No, it was the terrible consequences of broadcasting a recipe live.

In fairness, some of these recipes were straightforward and mercifully brief. But for some reason, they often tended to take a wrong turn into the surreal—something best captured in a novelty tune by William Bolcom and Joan Morris entitled "Lime Jell-O Marshmallow Cottage Cheese Surprise," a concoction that also includes:

[…]
slices of pimento
(You won't believe your eyes)
All topped with a pineapple ring
And a dash of mayonnaise,
My vanilla wafers 'round the edge
Will win your highest praise.

Nobody listening at home or in their car, of course, was in a position to stop what they were doing, find paper and a pen, and take dictation of a recipe already well in progress. Only later (sometimes weeks later) would these listeners call or write or email the show, requesting a copy of the recipe (which we never, never offered to provide, but always did).

The recipe we sent out would be based on my frantic shorthand (*2T mltd br/ drzl ovr ban/mack mxtr*). Back at my desk, it consumed an inordinate amount of time to decode the scribbles and then format a recipe for public distribution. *How's that recipe coming along, Big Guy?* my producer would query with a mischievous edge. *Don't forget you have to do that pre-tape in Studio D at four.*

For those of you who sent self-addressed, stamped envelopes all those years: thank you. But the make-work project of transcribing, printing, and mailing the recipe wasn't the only consequence. Once the four callers who had patiently endured the recipe recitation finally got on air and had their say about the real topic *du jour*, the inevitable follow-up call came.

Yes—that recipe that was on earlier? Grandma—on my father's side—used to make something very similar. But she always used smoked haddock instead of mackerel. And she used a Bundt pan.

Ah, I see. Well, thank you very—

And she always used unripe bananas, too. The ripe bananas would have ruined it. Would you like to hear my recipe?

Gingerbread Loaf

Vanilla Extract, Gingerbread Spice

MAKES 1 LOAF

This version of the famous French blend called *mélange pain d'épices* (gingerbread spices) is rich in ginger, allspice, cinnamon, and mace, with a touch of anise for that Gallic *je ne sais quoi*. The complex scent of this spice blend will evoke strong memories of traditional festive desserts. It enhances cookies, cakes, cheesecakes, muffins, and this simple loaf recipe.

3 tablespoons vegetable oil (such as canola)
¾ cup brown sugar
¼ cup molasses
2 eggs
½ teaspoon Vanilla Extract (see p. 9)
2 cups pastry flour
2 teaspoons baking soda
½ teaspoon salt
2 teaspoons Gingerbread Spice
¾ cup boiling water
1 teaspoon freshly grated orange zest

1. Preheat oven to 325°F (160°C).
2. Prepare an 8 × 4 × 2½-inch loaf pan with a little oil and dusted flour.
3. Combine vegetable oil and brown sugar in a bowl; beat well.
4. Add molasses and eggs, one at a time, beating well after each addition. Add Vanilla Extract.
5. Combine and sift dry ingredients and gradually stir into wet mixture, alternating with boiling water. Add orange zest.
6. Turn batter into loaf pan and bake for 45 minutes.

Janice Murray Gill's One-Kilogram Cheesecake

Vanilla Extract

MAKES 1 CAKE

On rare dinner occasions when I'm certain there'll be enough people to eat dessert—so that not a single morsel will remain to tempt me when they leave—I bake a cheesecake. Not just any cheesecake. It's known in the family as the "One-Kilogram Cheesecake," because it calls for four eight-ounce bricks of cream cheese.

Since I bake the recipe infrequently, I have to excavate it from a stack of food magazines in the closet. It's found in the inaugural issue of an excellent, but now defunct, Canadian publication called *Epicure*. The author of an 1980 article entitled "The Sweet Élan of Montréal" mentions she learned the cheesecake recipe from a woman named Rose Weiner, who trained as a pastry cook in Vienna before immigrating to the city four decades earlier (doing the math and reading between the lines, I suspect Rose had been fleeing the Nazis). The author writes, *Rose, a truly generous soul, was quick to donate cakes whenever her friends or neighbours needed a special dessert, big and rich enough for a dozen people, and everyone who tasted the heavenly cheesecake declared that it was without parallel.*

More than ten years after reading that article and recipe, I was in the CBC Radio studio following the one-hour *Maritime Noon* phone-in with Janice Murray Gill. Try to imagine, if you will, a five-foot four-inch version of Julia Child, without the trilling voice but with the same joie de vivre, jolly laugh, tart wit, encyclopedic knowledge of food, and desire to demystify cooking. Janice used to make the two-hour drive from River John on the Northumberland Strait, where she had been born and then retired with her husband Christopher. She was our expert guest on baking, because she'd written a legendary volume: *The*

Great Canadian Bread Book (*Faire Son Pain Soi-Même*, in the French edition). When someone would ask about eliminating the ½ teaspoon of salt from a recipe or substituting dried apple slices for fresh, she would remind them that "Cooking is Art, but Baking is Science," and then clearly explain how changing the aforementioned chemical components would alter the final compound.

In fact, Janice could field any culinary question, because in her years outside the Maritimes she had run a cooking school in Montréal, a city in which nobody would dare to merely dabble in such an enterprise. During that period she raised two boys, while appearing as a food commentator on radio, and writing newspaper columns and articles for magazines like *Canadian Living*, *Food and Wine*, and...*Epicure*.

Yes, the light bulb went on that day and I realized that Janice had written the article in *Epicure* with the famous One-Kilogram Cheesecake recipe. Janice died in the autumn of 2012, but her teachings and recipes—such as this one—live on.

Crust

½ cup sugar

1 cup all-purpose flour

1 teaspoon grated lemon rind

½ cup soft butter

1 egg yolk

Filling

2 ¼ pounds cream cheese (4 × 8 ounce blocks)

1 teaspoon grated lemon rind

½ teaspoon Vanilla Extract (see p. 9)

¾ cup honey

1 cup sugar

3 tablespoons all-purpose flour

¼ teaspoon salt

5 eggs; 2 yolks

¼ cup whipping cream

Topping

¼ cup honey

2 tablespoons blanched, slivered almonds

Method

Crust

1. Combine sugar, flour, and grated lemon rind in large bowl. Cut in butter (with pastry blender, two knives, or food processor) until mixture resembles cornmeal. Add egg yolk with fork.
2. Squeeze crumbs together with your fingers (it will be crumbly). Refrigerate 1 hour or freeze 20 minutes.
3. Preheat oven to 400°F (200°C).
4. Grease bottom and sides of 9-inch springform pan.
5. Spread ⅓ of crust over pan bottom. Flatten with rolling pin, bake 6 minutes. Let cool.
6. Carefully attach sides of pan. Roll remaining crust into 1-inch-thick ropes. Press onto the side, flattening and patting into place to form 2-inch-deep lining.
7. Refrigerate pan while making filling.

Filling

1. Place cream cheese in a bowl and beat with mixer until fluffy. Add grated lemon rind and Vanilla Extract. Continue beating while pouring honey in thin stream. Beat well.
2. Combine sugar, flour, and salt. Add mixture by the spoonful, beating continuously.
3. Beat in eggs, one at a time, then yolks. Add whipping cream and beat well. Scrape down sides of bowl and beat well again.
4. Pour mixture into prepared pan. Bake 8 minutes.
5. Lower heat to 200°F (93°C). Bake 1½ hours (or longer) until cake is set. Turn off oven. Leave cake in oven with door ajar for 30 minutes. Cool on wire rack.

Topping

1. Place pan containing the cheesecake on top of a large can or other firm support and gently remove sides. Transfer cheesecake, on the pan bottom, to a serving plate and refrigerate.
2. Warm a little honey until very thin, and lightly brush top of cake.
3. Toast almonds in a dry pan, occasionally turning until golden-brown. Sprinkle on cake, especially around edges, where cake may tend to shrink away from crust.
4. Serve chilled.

4

"Too Much"

In the summer of 2012, our family had the pleasure of billeting a couple of young guys from Cuba's National School of Music for a week. They were in the region performing gigs and taking part in workshops for a month—the fruit of a fascinating exchange between Nova Scotian and Cuban musicians, which had been growing for about fifteen years, aided and abetted by local sax man and teacher Jeff Goodspeed and a network of local volunteers.

Yadier, the bassist, was a showman: a tall, grinning extrovert who was always bouncing off the walls. Roberto, the trombonist, moved with the deliberation of an ancient tortoise. Both had gracious, impeccable manners. And while they were just teenagers, they were both professional-level musicians. How professional? One of their classmates, a pianist who'd been scheduled to come on the trip to Nova Scotia, had been hired at the last minute by Wynton Marsalis for an Afro-Cuban jazz project. What's equally amazing is that a percussionist classmate stepped in to play the demanding keyboard role for the Maritime tour. And he nailed it.

I had a hard time imagining what it must have been like to observe the relative luxury and comfort of Canadian middle-class life through the eyes of Yadier and Roberto. They had been separated from the North American mainland by 150 kilometres and a stupidly punitive relic of Cold War politics that predated their parents. And what did they see? Flat-screen HDTVs, pointless lawns, hulking SUVs, and fast-food strips. Perfectly functional chairs and cupboards tossed to the sidewalk on garbage day.

But it wasn't those symbols of affluence that got to them.

On the last day of their trip, Yadier and Roberto wanted to make one last excursion to a place their bandmates had told them about: Dollarama. I like Dollarama. It provides necessities at an affordable price. Nobody forces you to buy the trashy knick-knacks on the far-right aisles. I drove Yadier and Roberto down to the Dartmouth store and waited near the cash. After about five minutes, Yadier returned wide-eyed and, for once, not smiling. He was shaking his head anxiously. *Too much*, he said, *Too much!* He had simply been overwhelmed by the sensory overload of rows and rows of fully stocked shelves, jammed with everything from soup bowls to tacky decorations. He simply had never experienced so much choice. He had never experienced so much...stuff.

That December, I found myself thinking a lot about the look on Yadier's face. Like all retailers, I was preparing for my busiest month of the year. I'm happy to see an increase in sales, of course, and I'd ordered extra spice kits because they're popular gifts. I was consoled by the fact that the products I sell were purchased from growers at a fair price and destined for actual consumption—not for a box of unused toys or a closet of unworn clothes.

But I'm still ambivalent about it. The tradition of purchasing Christmas gifts is reinforced on so many levels by so many millions of dollars of paid advertising (and free "news" features tracking every twitch of seasonal consumer behaviour) that anyone who tries to resist it has to sail through powerful headwinds for weeks. In the malls, you feel the rising tide of anxiety: getting the right stuff, getting enough stuff, and getting stuff beyond that. Trying not to think about whether you can afford it. Or what compels you to go through this joyless annual ritual they call the "joyful season."

These aren't original thoughts. They've been voiced for generations. And people here in the so-called "First World" have been searching for alternatives to buying-for-the-sake-of-buying—from making charitable donations to creating their own gifts for loved ones. But how we resolve the push-pull of the season is something we need to negotiate—not just internally, but in an honest dialogue with friends and family, the people tied to us in murky mutual expectations of gift-giving, of card-sending, of party-going.

Good luck. And think of Yadier.

Caribbean Black Beans and Cornbread

Jerk Spices,
Jamaican or
Trinidadian Curry

Serves 6

Cuban cuisine doesn't tend to include a lot of spicing or heat. But the black beans, tomatoes, onions, and red pepper in this recipe are all staples in the Cuban kitchen, and the addition of other Caribbean spice blends works perfectly.

The Jerk Spices blend is a hot Jamaican spice rub containing allspice, habanero, thyme, shallot, mace, and West Indian bay leaf. Jamaican and Trinidadian curries are strong on the local aromatics (allspice, mace, dried ginger) but also include the turmeric introduced by East Indian settlers. The Trinidadian Curry also has a distinctive ingredient: chickpeas.

2 tablespoons olive oil
1 medium onion, chopped
1 sweet red pepper, diced
2 cloves garlic, minced
1 (15 ounce) can black beans, rinsed and drained
1 (15 ounce) can diced tomatoes (juice included)
1½ cups frozen corn
mild chilies to taste (see Chili Heat Scale, p. 56–57)
2 teaspoons Jerk Spices

Cornbread
½ cup all-purpose flour
½ cup cornmeal
1 tablespoon sugar
¼ teaspoon salt
1¼ teaspoon baking powder
⅔ cup coconut milk
2 tablespoons olive oil

1. Preheat oven to 350°F (180°C). Lightly oil an 8-inch square baking dish.
2. Heat oil in a large frying pan. Add onion and red pepper; cook until soft. Add garlic and cook 1 minute longer. Add black beans, diced tomatoes, corn, and chilies and heat through. Add Jerk Spices to taste. Spread in prepared baking dish.
3. In a bowl, whisk together flour, cornmeal, sugar, salt, and baking powder. Add coconut milk and olive oil. Stir until just combined—do not over mix. Spread batter over bean mixture with spatula.
4. Bake uncovered for 30 minutes, or until topping is lightly browned and toothpick inserted in centre of cornbread comes out clean. Let stand for 5 minutes before serving.

5

The Garden: An Urban Drama

The neighbourhood garden was one of those plots you hatch in winter when you're trying to take your mind off…winter.

CHARACTERS: Residents of three households connected by a backyard path.

ACT 1: A January evening. Six co-conspirators are sitting around after a potluck, imagining warmer days to come. Wine is involved.

It's decided that the crime against agriculture will go down in the "high and dry" end of my yard (which rapidly slopes away to the "low and swampy" end). Why? It gets the most light of the three properties. We reasoned that before the elms and beeches on the eastern side of my yard leafed out, the soil in that sweet spot would be warmed by early spring sunlight. Brilliant. And by the time the trees did leaf out, the sun would be high enough to pour its rays onto the garden for most of the day. Excellent.

The next stage of plotting for this incredibly small agricultural co-op was easy. Some people are fortunate enough to have a friend with a pile of well-rotted manure. In our case, we were fortunate enough to have (bilingual Canadian pun alert) "a guy like Guy." He can generate 3-D drawings on his computer. Call it over-engineering if you will, but Guy designed a compact, 12 × 12-foot terraced garden, complete with a pathway allowing easy weeding.

We dedicated a 4 × 4-foot square in the northwest corner to our most ambitious long-term dream: asparagus. Below that, there was a path on its east and south sides and then a larger L-shaped garden below that, suitable for tomatoes, beans, peas, leeks, an eggplant (just for kicks), and border herbs. Beautiful.

ACT 2: Spring 2011. Week after week of rain and chilly temperatures. No sunbeams streaming through those leafless trees. Moss thrives.

It was the grey, cold Victoria Day weekend before we caught two consecutive days dry enough to cut lumber and assemble the garden boxes out on Don and Carol's deck. Another week passed before we got the truckload of organic soil mix to fill the raised beds.

Then, for most of the month of June, it rained.

There was loose talk of turning the garden into rice paddies. Maybe a cranberry bog. Eventually (by Canada Day), the soil drained enough for us to put in transplants and seeds. Things grew slowly. At night, we could hear slugs chanting raucous marching songs as they advanced over the cold, damp earth towards the feeble plants. Mornings, the "garden" looked like a post-apocalyptic wasteland.

ACT 3: Late July 2011. Well, post-apocalyptic movies always involve hardy survivors and rebirth, so….

The soil finally warmed up and dried out. The organic soil mix turned out to be rich in nitrogen, so the tomato transplants gorged themselves and sprouted a forest of leaves, followed by blossoms and—marvel of marvels—tomatoes. The asparagus, now transformed into tall, airy ferns, nodded in approval.

Then, in the now-familiar one-step-forward, two-steps-back pattern that haunted our enterprise, we learned about blossom-end rot. Farmers and experienced gardeners: please try to stop snickering at this inevitable turn of events.

After pitching the "rotters" into the compost and finding ourselves paying much closer attention to supermarket flyers featuring cheap Canadian vegetables, we hit a surprisingly decent stretch of hot August weather. Suddenly, the three households turned from despair towards wondering how quickly we could deal with a burgeoning crop of ripening tomatoes: about six varieties, from sprays of Tiny Tims and miniature yellow plum tomatoes to beefsteaks big enough to knock down candlepins.

As much as this Hollywood-worthy reversal of fortunes in Act 3 cheered us up, I regret to inform you that there will be no transparency regarding the cost-benefit analysis of this project. We didn't dare do a cost-benefit analysis. That's how you discover such economic grotesques as the thirty-dollar tomato. But the tomatoes, whatever their unit cost, all found a home on our plates and in our bottles of salsa. And in the 2012 and 2013 sequels, the asparagus showed they could overwinter and send up more shoots than the year before.

So let's raise a glass to the creative hothouse of the Canadian winter and the summertime drama it inspires.

Roasted Tomato Salsa

Oaxaca or Tlalelolco Rub, Dried Chilies

MAKES 3 CUPS

Some Mexican Rubs, although more often used on meats, do wonders for salsa. The Oaxaca Rub is a blend of guajillo and ancho chilies, dried garlic, sea salt, thyme, and Mexican oregano. The Tlalelolco Rub has smoky aromas—thanks to the chipotle chili—as well as some heat from the arbol chili. It is rounded out with sea salt, allspice, epazote (an indigenous Mexican herb that aids in digestion), and culinary avocado leaves. The roasting intensifies the flavours as the sugars in the tomatoes begin to caramelize.

12 small tomatoes
1 (*or more*) fresh chili pepper(s)
2 (*or more*) cloves garlic, unpeeled
1 onion, quartered
1½ tablespoons olive oil

2 teaspoons (*or more*) Tlalelolco or Oaxaca Rub
3 tablespoons fresh lime juice
¼ cup chopped fresh cilantro *or* other herb
¼ teaspoon salt (rubs already contain sea salt)
Optional: rehydrated dried chili for a thicker salsa (pasilla or chipotle for a smoky flavour, or ancho negro or ancho rojo for a more complex flavour and mild heat)

1. Slice tomatoes in two; remove cores.
2. Stem chili pepper(s). Slice in two, lengthwise (To reduce heat, deseed and devein. Protect hands with plastic gloves if working with fresh, hot peppers).
3. Preheat broiler. Place tomatoes and chili(es) skin-side-up in medium baking dish with garlic, onion, and drizzled olive oil.
4. Broil 5–10 minutes, checking often, until outsides of vegetables are charred. Remove from heat.
5. In food processor, or by hand, coarsely chop charred vegetables. Transfer to a medium bowl. Add rub of choice, optional salt, lime juice, and chopped cilantro or other fresh herb.
6. Cover and refrigerate for up to 2 weeks, or process according to standard canning instructions for salsas.
7. *Optional*: soak 1 dried chipotle, pasilla, or ½ an ancho negro or ancho rojo in hot water and add to other vegetables when you chop or process them.

Recipe provided by Allrecipes.com

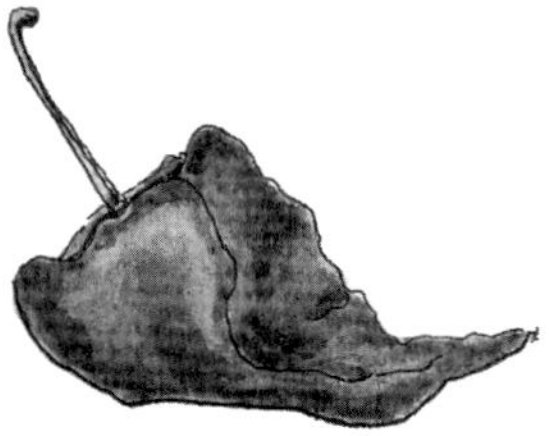

ancho chili

6

Everything, All The Time

This is the wishy-washiest record collection I've ever seen.

My friend was shaking his head as he flicked through the twenty or so LPs I owned. It was the summer of 1971 and I was, unbelievably, the assistant director of a combination youth hostel/drug crisis centre in Saint John called the Awarehouse. I had a room in the Victorian-era building, which, in the peculiar evolution of surplus public property, had been home to the well-dressed denizens of the city's school board the year before.

That summer, the Awarehouse was the government-funded response to two major social phenomena of the time: It was a temporary home (two-night maximum) for an entire generation of young people who'd set off hitchhiking across Canada (beds and soup kitchen, upstairs), and temporary refuge for young people who'd ingested who-knows-what combination of street drugs (dimly lit room with a big comfy couch and chair, no windows, downstairs). I was in between, on the second floor, and all my earthly possessions could still fit in one room.

Man, Herb Alpert and the Tijuana Brass? My friend was incredulous. It was still a time when my music collection was small enough that I could remember the circumstances of buying each piece of vinyl. That one was from a drugstore in Truro. Buying it had seemed like a good idea at the time: the end of a long afternoon in 1968 at a tavern in Bible Hill called the Ponderosa. Aesthetic decisions are subjective, and vulnerable to the influence of draught beer.

Hendrix, OK—but this other stuff.... My friend was appalled at the lack of definition in these records, the absence of any sign that I was trying to be in the vanguard of changing musical taste. But my record collection spanned that fascinating decade when popular music seemed to be an endless series of earthquakes. I'd begun buying 45s and LPs even before I had anything to play them on. By the time I did, a new artist or band would break on through to the other side of public consciousness every week, sounding unlike anything ever heard before. The Top 40 reflected this upheaval—the audio equivalent of those geological outcroppings where ancient and younger formations find themselves fused together. In the days before "narrowcasting," Mitch Miller and his Sing Along Chorus coexisted with "Peppermint Twist"; the schmaltzy trumpeter Bert Kaempfert with the incendiary Ray Charles.

While radio programmers tried to sort this out by designing stations that appealed to segments of musical taste ("Lite Rock," "Classic Rock," "Country," etc.), the burgeoning record-buying public began pursuing their own idiosyncratic interests, which led to collections like mine. I guess it had never crossed my mind to align my collection with the "now" and denounce anything that wasn't hip that month. I couldn't throw out old records any more than I could deny my musical roots. Only a few years had passed since I'd been singing in church choirs and playing marches in the school band. By 1971 the cultural chasm between Top 40 contemporaries Crosby, Stills and Nash and The Carpenters was immense, but the harmonies of each could make me sit back and utter the most common word of the era: *Wow!*

The wishy-washy record collection has since been joined by walls of wishy-washy cassettes and stacks of wishy-washy CDs. It now coexists with downloads and streaming audio. So what? Just because a chef on YouTube can show you how to make mayonnaise, should you chuck out your old cookbooks? If Korean food is hot this season, should you stop eating Italian? Of course not. It's exhausting and pointless to try to be on the cutting edge, which is a very narrow habitat for a human. And, short of developing dementia, erasing past enthusiasms isn't anything you can do consciously. As the noted philosopher Willie Nelson once said, in explaining his difficulties with the IRS: "There are no ex-wives—only additional wives." Life is layered like geological strata. Nothing really goes away. Cherish it all, and make no apologies.

Chili Con Carne

Chili Spice Blend

SERVES 8

At the same time that I was beginning to accumulate my wishy-washy collection of LPs, I was starting to add one recipe at a time to my small culinary repertoire: spaghetti sauce, seafood chowder, corned beef hash, omelettes, and burgers. There was also a basic chili, with fatty ground chuck and a few hits of Tabasco. Eventually I graduated to a chili that used chunks of beef and pork and more flavourful seasonings, like this recipe.

The Chili Spice Blend from the Spice Trekkers includes no fewer than five flaked chilies (New Mexico mild, chipotle grande, ancho, arbol, chimayo) and a touch of Kurdish Isot Pepper (very untraditional) as well as dried garlic, oregano, anise, bay leaf, thyme, and allspice. Don't wait for the Super Bowl to make this hearty, sociable dish.

2 tablespoons vegetable oil
1 large onion, chopped
1 red pepper, chopped
1–2 tablespoons Chili Spice Blend (*or* to taste)
2 pounds beef and/or pork in ½-inch cubes
4 cloves garlic, chopped
1 (28 ounce) can diced tomatoes

1 (28 ounce) can crushed tomatoes
2–4 cups black beans*
1 cup frozen corn kernels
salt to taste

Garnish
grated cheddar
chopped, fresh coriander

***A Note on Black Beans**

If using dried black beans, quick-soak them.

To make 3 cups of beans for the chili, generously cover 1 cup dried black beans with water. Bring to a boil, remove from heat, and let sit for 1 hour. Drain, cover with fresh water, and simmer until tender (45–90 minutes, depending on freshness of the dried beans).

Or, use 1–2 cans of tinned black beans (your preference). Drain and rinse before adding to chili.

1. Sauté onion and red pepper in medium-hot vegetable oil for 5 minutes.
2. Add Chili Spice Blend and cook for 3 minutes.
3. Add cubed meat and garlic and cook, stirring constantly, for 3 minutes.
4. Add diced tomatoes, crushed tomatoes, and salt. Simmer for ½ hour.
5. Add black beans and combine well. Check the flavours. Add more Chili Spice Blend or salt if desired.
6. Cook mixture for ½ hour so that beans acquire the flavours from the chili.
7. Add corn kernels and heat thoroughly.
8. Serve with grated cheddar and/or fresh coriander.

7

The Nose Knows

The most important tip in choosing spices? The tip of your nose.

That's how I'd paraphrase the liberating advice from Philippe and Ethné de Vienne when they conducted spice workshops in Halifax and Dartmouth a few years ago. Despite the specialized knowledge they've gained over decades spent hunting spices around the world, blending them in their Montréal facility, and cooking with them, the message from the founders of Spice Trekkers/Épices de Cru was that simple. You could feel everyone in the room relax: instant demystification.

That's why I often greet newcomers to my table in the Historic Farmers' Market by inviting them to take a whiff of a spice blend or a pepper. Then I'll ask, *What does that make you think of?* Or, *What do you think this would work with?* (And for the grammarians out there, is a preposition a suitable word to end a sentence with?)

There are a few blends that almost automatically make the whiffers blurt out *Christmas!* For a holiday whose traditions were developed in Europe and North America, it's interesting that these Yuletide-evoking spice blends are actually classics of Middle Eastern cuisine. (More on those later.)

But this makes me recall a conversation with a friend who felt his children had reached an age when it was time to start gently ratcheting down some of the household traditions surrounding Christmas—from decorations and feasting to the expanding networks (and expense) of gift exchanges. These had been accumulating and escalating for the better part of twenty years.

When it comes to revising the Christmas template, a de-escalation of expectations might happen. Some new traditions might evolve. But no matter how things change, some "pre-reform" memories will always be locked in his children's brains, waiting to be triggered by scents: baking gingerbread, a pine bough, or mulling cider.

One of the most famous passages in French literature is the following:

> *But when from a long distant past nothing subsists, after the people are dead, after the things are broken and scattered, taste and smell alone, more fragile but enduring, more insubstantial, more persistent, more faithful, remain poised a long time, like souls, remembering, waiting, hoping, amid the ruins of all the rest; and bear unflinchingly, in the tiny and almost impalpable drop of their essence, the vast structure of recollection.*

It's from a scene in Marcel Proust's *Remembrance of Things Past* (also known as *In Search of Lost Time*), in which the narrator takes a bite of a *madeleine*—that lemony, buttery cookie traditionally baked in the seashell-shaped indentations of a special pan. One sniff, one nibble, and his childhood comes roaring back. Jonah Lehrer, author of *Proust Was a Neuroscientist*, calls this passage "prophetic," because when it was being written, shortly before the First World War, anatomists considered the brain "three pounds of mysterious mush." According to Lehrer, Proust's insight that "our senses of smell and taste bear a unique burden of memory" was eventually borne out by science.

Odours and tastes head straight to the hippocampus, where long-term memories are formed. Hearing, sight, and touch, however, take a neural detour, stopping at the thalamus before resuming their journey to the hippocampus. Perhaps there's some shrinkage of sensation in the course of the trip, who knows? Ask your friendly neighbourhood neuroscientist. And consider this comparison: the sight of a balsam fir in the forest doesn't necessarily make you think of Christmas. But walk into a warm room on a winter night and catch the scent of a few of its boughs. Before you've even seen them, your brain will have already taken you on a sentimental olfactory journey.

Getting back to those blends whose aromas conjure up Christmas, it's hard to beat Lebanese Seven Spice (pepper, fenugreek, cassia, allspice, clove, nutmeg, and ginger). Aside from giving an authentic depth of flavour to keftas, shawarmas, lamb, rice pilafs, or grilled chicken, it's an extremely versatile blend to have on hand if you want to perk up a holiday classic without abandoning traditional flavours, cooking aromas, and tastes. Think about gingerbread cookies, mulled wine, or an aromatic rub on baked ham to mention a few. But only after you've had a sniff.

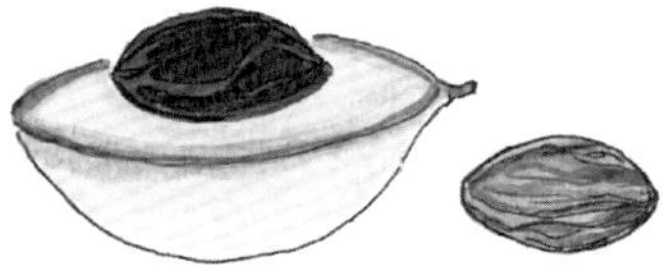

nutmeg

Bread Pudding with Lebanese Seven Spice

Lebanese Seven Spice, Vanilla Extract

MAKES 8 SERVINGS

Bread puddings are a favourite comfort food: versatile, easy to make, and supremely tasty. Lebanese Seven Spice is the most popular blend in Lebanese cooking. While it is mostly used with meats and rice pilafs in the Middle East, it works deliciously in apple crumbles and pumpkin pies, mulled cider, and muffins.

Also, you can make your own pure Vanilla Extract for this or any recipe from vanilla pods.

6 slices day-old bread
2 tablespoons butter, melted
½ cup currants *or* raisins (optional)
4 eggs, beaten
2 cups milk
⅓ cup sugar
1 teaspoon ground Lebanese Seven Spice
1 teaspoon Vanilla Extract (see p. 9)

1. Preheat oven to 350°F (175°C).
2. Break bread slices into small pieces. Place in 8-inch square baking pan.
3. Drizzle melted butter over bread.
4. If desired, sprinkle with currants or raisins.
5. In a bowl, combine eggs, milk, sugar, ground Lebanese Seven Spice, and Vanilla Extract. Beat until well-mixed. Pour over bread. Lightly push down with fork until bread soaks up egg mix.
6. Bake for 45 minutes, or until top springs back when lightly tapped.
7. Serve hot, with or without a drizzle of maple syrup.

Recipe provided by Allrecipes.com

8

Spice Therapy

It's not enough just to write a novel, launch an ambitious new business, or be an elite athlete any more. I'm sorry, but those accomplishments just don't cut it on their own. What you need is A Story.

I think it started innocently enough, with dust jacket blurbs on books. Before you had a chance to scan a few pages and decide whether you were reading the work of a writer or a mere typist, a publicist would have seized your attention by tossing out a list of the author's impossibly picaresque jobs: *Having spent time herding manatees on the Florida Coast, working as a sous-chef in a Sicilian trattoria frequented by Mafiosi, and guiding mercenaries through the landmine-riddled mountain passes of Kashmir, he felt it was time to write the novel that had been gestating in his imagination for so many years....* The novel, as it turns out, features a thinly disguised version of the author trying to figure out why his girlfriend left him for that damned jock in sophomore year.

The need for a distracting story is most pervasive in sports. Right now, there are television crews shooting "stories" of athletes who'll be competing in the 2014 Winter Olympics. Again, it's not enough to be the best Grand Slalom skier in your country, aiming to be best in the world. What you need is something in your young life to create what the ancient Greeks knew to be a key to persuading people to buy your message: pathos, the appeal to the emotions of your audience.

Pathos is that part of the story which serves as the cue for the tinkly piano music and soft-focus lens, followed by a close-up of the misty-eyed athlete talking about the loss of a loved one. I can imagine a frantic TV producer, though, confronted with a competitor who seems to have led a charmed life, untouched by loss.

> *You must have experienced some personal…tragedy.*
> *Like when the cat ate my gerbil?*
> *No! The death of a person who was close to you! How about Grandma?*
> *No, she's still alive.*
> *OK—how about Great-Grandma?*
> …
> Paydirt. Roll the Great-Grandma bit:
> *I never met her, but I know that when I'm out there on that mountain, she'll be looking down on me and guiding me through those gates.*
> *Thanks, kid. Heartwarming story. It's a wrap.*

But never mind authors and athletes, it turns out that even someone in the spice trade needs a story. I was struck by an acute attack of Story Envy when I read about Lev Sercarz, the hot new spice merchant in the Big Apple who got the full *New York Times* magazine treatment. He is impossibly exotic, of course (of "German-Belgian-Transylvanian-Tunisian stock"). While I was working in an office, hunched over a computer or a microphone for years, he was cooking with the Israeli Defense Forces, "sautéeing two hundred chicken cutlets on a propane stove in Lebanon while Hezbollah rockets whooshed overhead."

Sercarz's New York spice shop is so über-cool it's open only twelve hours a week. Like Dior or Versace, he unveils his "Spring/Summer Collection" of blends (the most recent event was called "The Tip of the Sword" for some inexplicable reason). And he certainly doesn't call his spice blends anything so consumer-friendly as "Madras Curry" or "Steak Rub"; he gives them names like "Shabazi," "Kibbeh," and "Mishmish." This would be cute if he were naming cats in the privacy of his loft, but spice blends? C'mon.

Never mind. When you set out to take Manhattan, you need to build mystique. In fact, Lev is not a mere hawker of cumin and fenugreek, like *moi.*

He is a spice *therapist*, y'all. The more I read, the more I identified with the author of the article, Alex Halberstadt, who described himself as "a home cook of middling talent and curiosity." At one point, we cross into "The Emperor's New Clothes" territory as Sercarz uses a few of the writer's autobiographical details to concoct a spice blend he names "Stavia." Halberstadt initially finds it "homely," but after a few days of following his spice therapist's instructions to "put it onto nearly everything," it begins to work strange neurological wonders. When Sercarz asks about "Stavia," Halberstadt says he wasn't absolutely sure he liked the taste, but added: "it made me remember odd, embarrassing things about my childhood." The spice therapist takes this as a profound compliment.

So if you'll excuse me, I think I'll ignore the mundane tasks of making my weekly spice order, updating my newsletter's mailing list, and testing new recipes. I obviously need to begin crafting My Story.

For starters, I'm so cool, I only open for six hours a week. But the recipe on the next page is for people who are more interested in flavour than mystique.

Leek, Yoghurt, and Mint Soup

Aleppo Pepper, Mint

SERVES 4

As its name suggests, this fruity, flavourful pepper is associated with the Aleppo region of Syria, but it's also grown in other parts of the Middle East. It has a noticeable amount of heat (5/10 on the relative heat scale), but that's much less than, say, a habanero (9/10) (see Chili Heat Scale, p. 56–57). Seeds are extracted before the pepper is ground. It's especially good in marinades, and just a sprinkle will give a piquant and colourful accent to steamed vegetables. Or you can place a tiny bowl of Aleppo pepper on the table for dinner guests to add as they wish.

Since mint is one of the earliest spring perennial herbs, its appearance reminds me to make this delicious soup.

3 tablespoons olive oil
3 tablespoons butter
2 large leeks, roots and green leaves removed
1 tablespoon Aleppo pepper
½ cup chopped fresh mint *or* 1 tablespoon dried mint
2 cups chicken broth
salt and pepper, to taste
1½ cups plain yoghurt
1 egg
2 tablespoons flour
butter for garnish

1. In a heavy-bottomed pan, heat oil and butter over medium heat.
2. Halve leeks lengthwise, then rinse, chop, and add to pan when butter begins to bubble. Sauté 10 minutes, stirring from time to time.
3. Cover and cook gently for 25 minutes to allow leeks to steam, not brown.
4. Add broth, Aleppo pepper, mint, salt, and pepper. Simmer for 5 minutes.
5. Whisk together yoghurt, egg, and flour in a small bowl.
6. Lower heat and add yoghurt mixture to pan. Stir constantly to heat through, but without allowing it to come to a boil.
7. Heat butter for garnish in a small pan, cooking until lightly browned. On each serving of soup, drizzle a little browned butter, and serve.

9

Marking Time

Calendar years, school years, fiscal years—no matter how you measure twelve months, they blitz by with alarming speed. Every December I notch another birthday. Considering its substantial number, however, an attractive alternative presents itself: measuring my time from now on in spice years (starting when I first set up a table at the Historic Farmers' Market in December 2010).

Greeks have a clever excuse for an annual celebration that doesn't actually acknowledge the passage of time: Name Day. Since most Greeks are named after saints, everyone named George/Georgia parties, regardless of age, on the feast day of their saint. And since there's a small pool of saints' names, you're sure to have lots of celebratory company.

December 6th—St. Nicholas Day—is my eldest son's name day. We always send a chocolate letter "N" to him in Montréal, but when he was much younger there would be a small gift, too. In 1989 I bought him a CD by the Canadian group Men Without Hats. They'd had a big pop hit with "Safety Dance," but the title of their new album included an intriguing pun on the band's name: *The Adventures of Women and Men Without Hate in the 21st Century*. It sounded hopeful, almost utopian.

The first single was an infectious rocker called "Hey Men." But unlike thousands of previous songs written by guys with guitars and amplifiers, the lyrics contained notions that were light years away from *Aw, baby, you know what I want/And you want it, too!* I had never heard a male singer toss out a line as Jungian as *I got a woman inside*, or belt out a chorus with such a blunt challenge to his fellow men: *Hey men/Quit knockin' your children 'round/Hey men/Quit mowin' your women down/Cause it's all in the way/That you look at who you are.*

The 1970s had seen Maritime communities make their first steps towards acknowledging male violence towards women and children by establishing emergency shelters in residential areas. It hadn't been easy. Potential neighbours used zoning bylaws to keep these houses as far away from them as possible. Shelters were a too-uncomfortable truth about what happens in every town and city. By 1989, however, these shelters had become a part of many communities.

But what about changing the attitudes that led to this violence? When I gave the CD to Nick, I remember feeling that if a mainstream band like Men Without Hats could release a hugely popular song with the pointed lyrical content of "Hey Men," perhaps it was a sign that the men and women of his generation were on the threshold of a world with safer, more peaceful relationships.

That night, fourteen young women were shot to death at Montréal's École Polytechnique.

From that St. Nicholas Day forward, December 6th would carry a painful historic burden (yes, it's already burdened with being the anniversary of the Halifax Explosion). In 2011, people (that would be women *and* men) commemorated the victims of the Montréal Massacre at an anniversary gathering on Parliament Hill. The group felt betrayed by the government's decision to do away with the Long-Gun Registry Act, which had followed from the 1989 tragedy.

I elaborated on "people" as "women *and* men" above, because of another news item of that same week in 2011. The Bank of Canada announced it was removing The Famous Five—the female activists who succeeded in having women included in the legal definition of "people" in 1930—from our fifty-dollar bill. They were replaced by a picture of a coast guard vessel. So while

I head into a new spice year every December and the pages on the calendar continue to turn, I still marvel at the ability of our species to turn back certain pages, quite selectively.

Over the years, I took part in many December readings of Dickens's *A Christmas Carol.* Thanks to the work of Judy Maddren, one of CBC Radio's finest announcers, it became a nationwide vehicle for local charitable fundraisers. The book, written in the 1840s, features those symbols of the working poor: the Cratchit family. The story continues to chill, especially when we recall that we've missed the deadline for dealing with the same problems in our modern era: the 1989 all-party resolution in the House of Commons to eliminate child poverty by 2000, for example.

There are too many injustices still around us, perpetrated upon individuals and groups. There are too many distractions keeping us from focusing our attention on even *one* for long enough to make a difference. Let's take time—especially once the manic month of December rolls around—to reflect on what concrete things we can do to help remedy them over the next twelve months.

cinnamon

Whenever events in the world outside seem too disturbing, the first step towards regaining a sense of peace can be sharing a meal and conversation with family or close friends, who are always a reminder of what's good about life. At times like this, the phrase "comfort food" takes on a heightened meaning. I find this recipe especially comforting.

Lamb Shanks Tajine

Tajine Spice Blend

Serves 4

Tajine Spices are aromatic and flavourful, the perfect exotic accent for this classic North African dish. They include cumin, chilies, coriander, ginger, turmeric, guinea pepper, kentjur (a rhizome like ginger), mace, white pepper, long pepper, mint, cardamom, cassia buds, black cardamom, cloves, cinnamon, allspice, bay leaves, lavender, rose petals, nigella, and fenugreek.

4 lamb shanks
2 tablespoons Tajine Spice Blend
2 tablespoons vegetable oil
4 prunes
2 carrots, chopped
2 onions, chopped
1 parsnip, peeled and cubed
1 (14 ounce) can plum tomatoes
2 cups water
1 cup orange juice
1 tablespoon garlic purée
1 tablespoon tomato paste
3–4 peppercorns, crushed
salt to taste

1. Preheat oven to 325°F (160°C). Coat lamb shanks with Tajine Spice. Blend and sear lightly in hot vegetable oil.
2. Place in large ovenproof pot. Add all other ingredients; stir to mix.
3. Cover and bake 1½–2 hours, until lamb is tender.
4. Add salt to taste and serve with Couscous (see next page).

Couscous

1 cup dry couscous

1 tablespoon olive oil

1 cup boiling water

Optional toppings: raisins, a pinch cinnamon, 1 teaspoon Couscous Blend

1. Put dry couscous in heatproof bowl or saucepan.
2. Toss with olive oil to lightly coat couscous grains.
3. Add boiling water. Cover and let sit 10 minutes.
4. Remove lid and toss with a fork to fluff couscous.
5. Top with garnish of your choice (raisins, cinnamon, or Couscous Blend).

10

Reality TV and Unreal Heat

When someone begins a conversation by saying, *I don't watch much TV*...the silent subtext is: *that makes me a more serious/intellectual/high-minded person than most other people*. It tends to stifle anyone who was thinking about launching a meaningful discussion of *Duck Dynasty*, *America's Next Top Model*, or *RuPaul's Drag Race*.

Anyway, there I was recently, going through a vigorous warm-up routine: gentle channel-surfing before self-composting into the couch for a deeply vegetative hour. It was the "top of the clock," so my thumb clicked through the opening sequence of a few dozen shows. Suddenly, an arresting image stopped me. The opening sequence of the reality show *Hairy Bikers* featured a close-up of a Bhut Jolokia: the infamous "Ghost Pepper." The gnarly little thing is the second-hottest chili pepper on Earth. According to Guinness World Records, it has been out-flamed by the Trinidad Moruga Scorpion, but given the variability of these hybrids and the competitiveness of botanists, who knows what'll be at the top of the pyre by the time you read this.

But there was the Bhut Jolokia on my TV, glistening on an innocent-looking pepper plant. As I mentioned, the show was entitled—in the what-you-see-is-what-you're-gonna-get style of naming reality shows—*Hairy Bikers*. On the History Channel. Yes, the History Channel. (As you might have noticed, the licensing of Canadian cable channels is so laughably pliable that it could just as easily have been on a sports or lifestyle or food channel.) The two Hairy Bikers had stopped at the home of a young Texan woman who grows Bhut Jolokia and other chilies, which she uses to make hot sauces. Since there are never any surprises on reality TV, the Hairy Bikers were levelled by a single nibble of the sweet-l'il-thang's Ghost Pepper.

I knew of the Bhut Jolokia ("poison chili" in Assamese), thanks to intrepid fans of heat who asked me to order some. One local heat freak steeps it in canola and injects it into a beef brisket, then uses *more* Bhut Jolokia in a dry rub. Then he smokes the brisket. Another makes a tincture by steeping Bhut Jolokia in vodka, and then adds a few drops to his Bloody Caesars. (Perhaps this should be a Bloody Nero, best sipped while watching Rome burn.) I'm starting to perspire just writing about this insanity.

Once I started stocking Bhut Jolokia, local heat aficionados came out of the asbestos-coated woodwork. I sell the dried peppers double-bagged, with explicit instructions to (a) wear latex or rubber gloves—and perhaps even a protective mask—when handling them, and (b) never, never, NEVER put any in someone's food (or drink) without telling them: it's not a joking matter.

The Bhut Jolokia was made for YouTube, with dozens of individuals (almost exclusively men) choking out live reportage of their self-inflicted pain. But the scariest video features a woman named Anandita Dutta Tamuli on a stage in Northeastern India, trying to surpass her 2008 world record of gobbling sixty fresh Bhut Jolokias. She fails, but then sets a new record by juicing two dozen into her eyes!

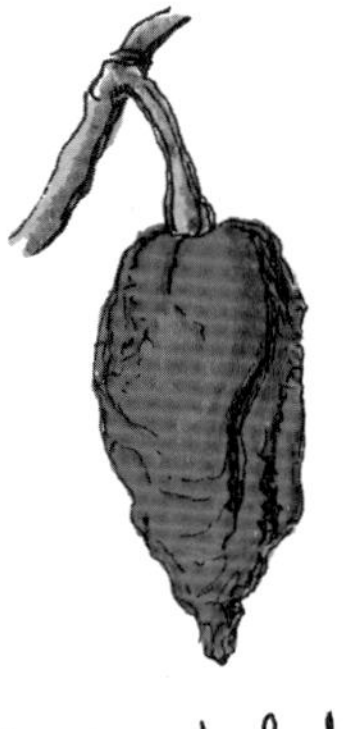

Bhut Jolokia

Shows that feature extreme eating (too hot, too fattening, too gross, too much) are my cue to change the channel, but they're increasing in number. The 2012 Factual Entertainment Industry convention in Washington, DC, *realscreen,* offered sessions such as "What Men Want." Here's the pitch:

> *Many of the top-rated factual franchises emerging over the past few years have been decidedly testosterone-oriented: witness the success of History's* Ice Road Truckers *and* Top Shot, *Discovery's* Deadliest Catch *and* Gold Rush: Alaska. *But beyond gadgets, gold, guns and derring-do, what elements keep males, a notoriously fickle audience, tuned in? What do men want to see in their non-fiction TV choices, and importantly, what don't they want to see?*

Take a wild guess.

And if you can't, hold the Bhut Jolokia and "non-fiction/factual/reality" shows, pass me the frozen yoghurt, and beam me up a well-scripted drama.

Getting Comfy With Dried Chilies

As you may have gathered, I'm not a fan of extreme heat. But some heat in my food—yes. As an ingredient, it can act like the single note that makes a musical chord more interesting. Far from the testosterone-laced world of *Hairy Bikers*, visitors to The Spiceman's table have noticed the growing variety of Mexican, Asian, Caribbean, and African chilies on offer. Chilies are a fascinating family, and part of everyday cuisine for men, women, and children in much of the world, so they're not exactly what I'd call "extreme" ingredients.

There are various heat scales for chilies. The Scoville scale, named after the American pharmacist who developed it, measures the level of *capsaicin*—the chemical compound that makes you "feel the burn." Bhut Jolokia registers about 1.4 million Scoville Heat Units (SHUs), which means you would have to dilute it to 1 part in 1.4 million parts water to make it undetectable. In the list below, I'll use a relative heat scale, which assigns Bhut Jolokia a 28/10. Chilies such as Thai, peri peri, and habanero are in the manageable range of 7/10 to 9/10 (50,000–350,000 SHUs).

Aside from escalating degrees of heat, chilies cover a remarkable spectrum of flavour, shape, size, and colour. Since they're dried, they offer many options, and you don't have to worry about them rotting—like that jalapeño you bought at the supermarket last month.

Chilies can be:

1. ground on their own or as part of a blend (snip off the amount you want to add),
2. rehydrated (soaked in water for a while),
3. dry-roasted in a pan to intensify the flavour,
4. added whole or flaked to stews or soups.

dried ancho chili

So whether you're a hairy Harley rider or a mild-mannered pedestrian, consider adding some chilies to your spice repertoire. Here are some chilies you should get to know if you're interested in exploring this often-neglected realm of taste.

Ancho Rojo	2/10	This large, mild-mannered Mexican chili is actually a poblano pepper; it's barely hot once you remove its seeds. Toast it in a dry pan and then open it to remove seeds and stems. Soak for 20 minutes in warm water or stock to make red salsas, recados (ground spice blends for sauces), and stews. It's also great in Chili Con Carne (see p. 36).
Reshampatti	5/10	The most common hot chili in Indian cuisine is this variety of cayenne. It's rather flavourless but colours dishes nicely if you first fry it in oil or ghee. (Ghee is clarified butter and has a higher "smoking point" than ordinary butter. It's available in Indian and Asian specialty stores, but now, more and more frequently, in supermarkets. It is usually sold in peanut butter-sized plastic containers and should be kept refrigerated.)

Szechuan Point Towards the Sun Pepper	5/10	Medium-hot, this pepper gets its name from the fact that it points towards the sun as it grows (unlike those droopy peppers). They're generally cut in two with scissors and partially de-seeded. At the start of traditional Szechuan stir-fries, throw as many as you need into hot oil to get the heat you want (along with Szechuan peppercorns and other whole chilies) for a few seconds until they brown, then add the other ingredients.
Chipotle Grande	5–7/10	This Mexican classic is used widely in commercial salsas, mayos, rubs, and many other products for its deep, smoky flavour.
Pasilla de Oaxaca	6/10	Medium-hot, very fruity, and lightly smoked, this chili can be used whole, like a bay leaf, in a stew. You can also use it flaked—the most efficient and versatile use—or toasted and rehydrated. It's a great addition to almost any dish—including chocolate sauces.
Thai	7/10	Small and very hot. Toss this pepper whole into the hot oil as you prepare a stir-fry.
Habanero	9/10	Synonymous with heat in Mexican cuisine, the habanero is also flavourful. It shows up in salsas and bean dishes in southern Mexico, and in pepper sauces, curries, and Creole dishes in the Caribbean. You can leave the seeds in the pod.
Peri Peri	9/10	This is a tiny, very hot African chili with a unique, citric flavour, used in African and Portuguese cooking and made famous in Portuguese grilled chicken. It's usually ground, but thanks to its size (similar to the Mexican piquin, or "Bird's-Eye," also 9/10), you can throw a few into stir-fries or stews. Make a quick peri-peri sauce by cooking the ground chili for a few minutes with vinegar, garlic, and salt.

II

Stayin' Alive

There's at least one community in the Maritimes whose private radio station broadcasts a daily feature that assures everyone in town will tune in and stop what they're doing, lest they miss a single detail. Newscasts, weather, and sports can't touch this item for all-demographic interest. Such a feature is the Holy Grail of radio programmers. But in case some other station manager might be tempted to copy it, I'm not certain how well it would fit between dance tunes by Rihanna and Drake. (Perhaps between selections by Mantovani and the Melachrino Strings and Orchestra, but not between Rihanna and Drake.)

The feature is...obituaries.

The obits are read not once, but twice, slowly and clearly. Perhaps this is because someone who is busy being defibrillated during the first reading wants assurance that he or she is still among the quick. Whenever I'm in this town, I always find this mid-day downer irresistible—something I feel I really shouldn't be doing, like when I ate those two shortbreads a few minutes ago.

So what's the opposite of this? I'm not sure. No radio station does a daily broadcast listing the names of those in the community who remain alive. Perhaps the closest to an opposite is an item about...what's good for you. But when I used to work at CBC, even those were problematic. Reports on the health benefits of ingesting some food product, its derivative, or one of its constituent enzymes, came streaming in to us through every communication medium known to humanity in the past half-century: mail, the pounding Telex machine, faxes, emails, banner ads on websites, and tweets. Promotional packages would occasionally arrive containing branded coffee mugs and

T-shirts (we gave them away to any guests who'd take them off our hands).

Often, a media release cited a "medical trial" or "scientific study" and invited us to interview a designated MD or Ph.D. on the significance of this "breakthrough." It was only through a critical reading and—in the case of more opaque prose—follow-up phone calls or web searches that you would learn there was a commercial interest involved. The research would have been funded by this same interest and, surprise: the "breakthrough" would tilt the listener/viewer/reader towards buying the product in question.

"Follow the money," indeed.

It's a miserable bind for the disseminators and amplifiers of information: the news media. There is independent, peer-reviewed research being done, but it costs money and it's increasingly rare. So for any given body of scientific research, who pays: the public or private sector? Whose interest is primary: the consumer or shareholders? And what of the news media? Are they developing specialists with the expertise to assess medical and scientific claims before broadcasting or publishing them? Or are they content with having something—anything—to fill two minutes of airtime or three column inches?

I'm not a member of the news media anymore. I sell spices. But my tendency towards skepticism hasn't disappeared. That's why I've been reluctant to promote the vast array of health claims attributed to eating certain spices: antioxidant, anti-inflammatory, cancer-preventing, bad cholesterol-lowering, good cholesterol-boosting, or some combination thereof. No study is ever definitive, and while I do subscribe to a few online feeds, I don't spend my days tracking the latest research on the health effects of including more spices in your food. But I believe you're all capable of sorting through health claims—wherever you may find them—for yourself. Just for kicks, look up a 2003 study entitled "Cinnamon Improves Glucose and Lipids of People With Type 2 Diabetes," published by the American Diabetes Association. Will it make you start spooning cinnamon onto your Ancient Grains cereal? Or does it raise more questions than it answers? And as always, full disclosure behind claims is paramount. For instance, I actually ate three shortbreads earlier. To the best of my recollection....

Chai Shortbread

Chai Spice Blend, Vanilla Extract, Cinnamon

MAKES ABOUT 2 DOZEN COOKIES

The Chai Spice Blend—cardamom, mace, fennel, clove, and black peppercorns—is one of the most fragrant. It is most often used to flavour tea (strong or weak) or hot milk.

This spiced variation on the classic little cookie will make it hard to go back to the way you made them before.

1 cup soft butter
½ cup icing sugar
2 teaspoons Vanilla Extract (see p. 9)
2 cups unbleached all-purpose flour
1½ tablespoons ground Chai Spice Blend
ground cinnamon to taste
¼ teaspoon salt
granulated maple sugar to sprinkle on shortbreads

1. Preheat oven to 350°F (180°C).
2. In a food processor, or with an electric beater, mix together butter, icing sugar, and Vanilla Extract. Add other ingredients and mix well.
3. Cover cookie sheet with parchment paper. Form cookies by hand, sprinkle with granulated maple sugar, and place on cookie sheet.
4. Bake 12–15 minutes.
5. Cool on rack.

Cassia Bud Cookies

Cassia Buds,
Vanilla Beans

MAKES ABOUT 18 COOKIES

Cassia buds, the unopened blossoms of the cassia tree, are the secret ingredient to better pickles, chutneys, and ketchups. The flavour is similar to cassia (or "false cinnamon" bark) but milder—almost headed towards nutmeg on the flavour spectrum. When you'd like a nuanced touch of cassia or cinnamon in a recipe, these delicate, clove-like buds are ideal. But they are also versatile and are well-suited to curries, poached fruit dishes, and apple desserts.

1 cup white flour
½ cup ground almonds
½ cup sugar
2 teaspoons ground cassia buds
1 vanilla bean
1 cup soft butter

1. Mix all dry ingredients.
2. Knead in soft butter.
3. Form 2 rolls (or more), wrap in cling wrap, and place in fridge for 1 hour.
4. Remove from fridge and cut rolls into ½-inch discs.
5. Bake at 320°F (160°C) for 20 minutes.

Delicious with a glass of chilled Nova Scotia Muscat, such as Domaine de Grand Pré's Vintner's Reserve, Jost's Eagle Tree, and Luckett Vineyards's Muscat.

12

Living on the Edge

When you see a TV ad that features people snowboarding off sheer cliffs, water-skiing through alligator-infested swamps, or kayaking over skyscraper-high waterfalls, do you feel you just can't "identify" with them?

You don't? Well I do. These are my kind of people. Our adrenal glands work harder than other people's hearts. Of course, I don't pursue any sports or pastimes that might cause—heaven forbid—injury, or even discomfort to my body. I believe that the sadistic sports slogan "No pain, no gain" was first whispered into the ear of a peasant by some brute stretching him on the rack. My favourite blues song is "Built For Comfort." Get the picture? No, there are other ways of living on the edge, of chasing the rush. Personally, I cook for friends.

One Saturday night, three neighbourhood households gathered for a pot-luck. I had offered to make dessert, a course that isn't my strong suit. Then again, this gang could be forgiven for wondering what my "strong suit" in the kitchen might be, given their previous experiences of my "cooking without a net." It's a testament to their loyalty that they still speak to me at all.

Where to start? Well, I'd enjoyed a cardamom rice pudding at a house party a few months earlier. I asked my friend who had prepared it if she'd send me the recipe, and she kindly did. The original was from *Elegant and Inspired: Vij's Indian Cuisine*, co-authored by the husband-and-wife team of successful Vancouver restaurateurs, Vikram Vij and Meeru Dhalwala. The recipe was the perfect delivery system for the Green Indian Cardamom I sell. So far, so good.

Official confession and apology: for the first and last time, I sent the unsuspecting subscribers to my newsletter a recipe whose original (a) I had amended and (b) I had not tested. Bad, bad Spiceman.

Context (a.k.a. defensive backtracking): Many years ago, I got in the habit of cooking rice in the top of a double boiler. Ever since, I haven't had to worry about it burning or sticking to the bottom of a pot. I know this sounds too cautious for a daredevil like me, but this method is very forgiving if the evening runs behind schedule (e.g. guests arrive late, police are called to quell a political argument that erupts while hors d'oeuvres are served, etc.).

But that wasn't reckless enough. When I found out I didn't have enough homogenized (3.25 per cent butterfat) milk, I threw caution to the wind and substituted 1 per cent. "Gee," I hear you say to yourself, "that sounds insane! What's it like to live so recklessly?"

Never mind. Now I was ready to test the latest evolutionary stage of the Cardamom Rice Pudding recipe I'd already sent to subscribers. I began to cook the rice-fat milk-skinny milk mixture in the top of a double boiler.

After sixty of the eighty suggested minutes had transpired (and far too much stirring, which kept me from what sounded like a really great time in the other room), it was obvious that the indirect heat of a double boiler wasn't enough. Or was it the 1 per cent milk instead of the 3.25 per cent? Who knows? There were too many terrifying variables. It was exactly the same as that bug-eyed moment when you see a ski jumper corkscrewing and backflipping through the Alpine air on the brink of losing control, and you gasp, "How will he ever land without breaking his neck?"

To make a long, humiliating story short, my neighbours waited a long time for dessert. I poured the mixture from the top of the double boiler into a saucepan. With the urging of one of the party (Guy, who is a much better cook), we added egg to thicken things, à la Greek Rice Pudding (*Rizogalo*). The ski jumper landed on his feet.

In a pathetic attempt at damage control, I emailed the friend who sent the original, unadulterated recipe, because, aside from my numerous failures in judgment, there was also something about the milk:rice servings ratio that seemed odd. She wrote back to tell me that she had followed the original to the letter twice, and, interestingly, gotten two different results. She wrote: *You might consider advising your readers that there have been inconsistent results with the recipe and you can't guarantee success.* Then she wisely added, *Making rice pudding is like experimenting with ice cream flavours—even if the combination attempted isn't wildly successful, the result is usually still pretty yummy.*

So, chastened, I sent out the twice-revised recipe for Cardamom Rice Pudding. It is inspired by Vij's recipe, but quite different. Also, my friend uses pistachios, which I think are a tastier complement than almonds.

But I'm clinging to the double boiler. Because I'm lazy, not chicken.

Cardamom Rice Pudding

Green Indian Cardamom

SERVES 6

Cardamom has a delightfully refreshing aroma and taste. In Indian cuisine, it is revered as the Queen of Spices and is added to curries, masalas, rice dishes, and desserts. In northern Europe it is used in traditional pastries; in the Middle East, to flavour coffee.

You can use the cardamom bud whole (crushed with the flat of a knife to open the pod to the seeds) or ground (husk retained or removed). Green Indian Cardamom, grown in the Cardamom Hills of Kerala state, is both aromatic and relatively rare.

Green Indian Cardamom

3 Green Indian Cardamom pods
1½ cups cooked basmati rice
3 cups homogenized milk, divided
¼ cup sugar (or to taste)
¼ teaspoon salt
1 egg, beaten
1 tablespoon butter
chopped almonds *or* unsalted pistachios to garnish

Optional: grated tonka bean: a hard-to-procure spice from the West Indies which the Spice Trekkers in Montréal have managed to source, and which I stock. It has notes of vanilla and cherry, and is excellent with custards, crème brûlée, and other dairy-based desserts. With its sweet aroma, it's not surprising that it's also used in the perfume industry.

1. Lightly pound Green Indian Cardamom pods. Peel off pods and discard, reserving seeds.
2. In top of a double boiler over simmering hot water, combine cooked rice, sugar, salt, cardamom seeds, and 2½ cups milk. Cook until thick and creamy, 20–30 minutes.
3. Stir in remaining ½ cup milk and beaten egg. Cook 3–4 minutes more, stirring constantly. Remove from heat and stir in butter.
4. Eat hot, warm, or cold. Sprinkle nuts and grated tonka bean over pudding just before serving. Wait until pudding is at room temperature before refrigerating.

13

Spaces We Love

I really enjoyed this book—care to borrow it?

This offer, usually made as a visiting friend is leaving, has kept my bookshelves light. The most frustrating thing, of course, is that you only lend the best books you've read, not the clunkers. And while my memory for certain things is good, I can never remember which friends I've pressed these books upon. My consolation is found in knowing the books that have taken this one-way trip have found a good home. To the conscientious souls who've read my books and returned them over the years, thank you. For the rest, it's not your fault. I must have drifted off for the second half of "Neither a borrower nor a lender be."

I'm not alone in this. A friend dropped by a few weeks ago for the latest installment of our ongoing dialogue about a non-urgent renovation project: my little old bathroom. Since our conversations always ramble beyond the topic at hand, he brought along a few books he thought I might be interested in. One was a cookbook (always a safe bet), but the second was an uncanny choice: *A Pattern Language: Towns, Buildings, Construction*. I hadn't laid eyes on it since the late 1970s, but I think of it often. That copy belonged to a dear friend in Saint John who specialized in rehabilitating older buildings (there are plenty there) to create affordable housing (there's never enough).

The book gives us two valuable things: a language to articulate the pleasurable sensations we get as soon as we enter a certain room, building, neighbourhood, or community, and a method for incorporating those time-honoured elements into towns, buildings, and construction, which will bring us joy. The tone, which announces each of the 253 patterns, is authoritative (and backed up by considerable research). Take pattern 159: "Light On Two Sides of Every Room." It states: *When they have a choice, people will always gravitate to those rooms which have light on two sides, and leave the rooms which are lit only from one side unused and empty.* Gee, that sounds right. But when it goes on to contrast the "social atmosphere" of such rooms, the authors use plain language to share their insight into how design affects the way we interact as humans: *Rooms lit on two sides, with natural light, create less glare around people and objects; this lets us see more intricately...to read the minute expressions that flash across people's faces...to understand one another.* For the room lit on one side: *the part furthest from the window is uncomfortably dark, compared with the part near the window...the glare which surrounds people's faces prevents people from understanding one another.*

Interestingly, the copy I was now borrowing was not the original one owned by my friend; he'd lent that to someone years ago (recognize the pattern?). His partner had tracked another one down and given it to him as a fiftieth-birthday gift, because, as she writes in the inscription, "You so often refer to how much you love this book."

I've been dipping into *A Pattern Language* every day, and it's given me many practical ideas for making my own house and yard more pleasurable (and to solve the problem posed by the tiny old bathroom). But since the book's scope extends far beyond rooms and personal property, it's no surprise that there's a pattern—number 46—entitled "Market of Many Shops," which is contrasted with the less desirable "supermarket" experience. The discussion includes the following: *The only way to get the human contact back, and the variety of food, and all the love and care and wisdom about individual foods which shopkeepers who know what they are selling can bring to it, is to create those markets once again in which individual owners sell different goods, from tiny stalls, under a common roof.*

Sound familiar? It's the pattern found in markets that have operated for centuries. The Medina of Marrakesh. Barcelona's La Boqueria. Aleppo's Al-Madina Souq (terribly damaged in 2012, during the Syrian civil war). The pattern describes the Saint John City Market, which I grew up with and which remains a magnetic shrine for "Johners" of all ages whenever they return to their hometown. Pattern 46 also describes the place I've inhabited on Saturday mornings since 2010: the naturally lit, stone-walled, covered upper courtyard of the Historic Farmers' Market (still known to many as "the Brewery Market") in Halifax. Thanks to my friend's loan of his beloved book, I now know why this space has always felt like home.

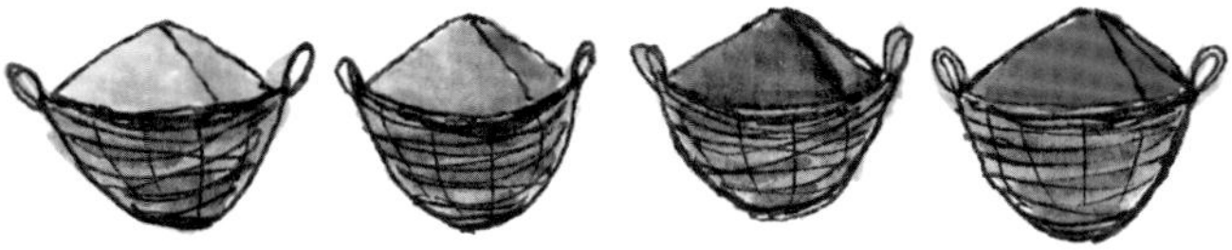

If there's a single spice blend I'd like to send home with someone who's never tried it, it's Ethiopian Berberé. If they use it once, I know they'll (a) be back for more, and (b) trust me to suggest other blends they've never tried (or perhaps even heard of). Berberé is a traditional Ethiopian blend, rather rare in Canada, but I believe it deserves to be as well-known as Madras Curry or Chili Spices. It's comprised of very aromatic, colourful, and delicious peppers and spices: three chili peppers, paprika, cardamom, ginger, coriander, clove, cinnamon, ajwain (a seed that tastes like thyme), fenugreek, allspice, and pepper. Altogether, they provide colour, aroma, and flavour. What more could you ask of a spice blend?

Berberé Roast Chicken

Ethiopian Berberé Blend

Serves 4

Ethiopian Berberé is often used in stewed-meat and poultry dishes, but try it with baked fish or roasted vegetables, too.

3 tablespoons ground Ethiopian Berberé Blend
4 cloves garlic, chopped
3 tablespoons melted butter
3 tablespoons fresh lemon juice
1 teaspoon salt
4 chicken breasts or 8 chicken thighs, skin on
4 onions, thickly sliced
¼ cup water

1. Preheat oven to 375°F (190°C).
2. Combine Ethiopian Berberé Blend, garlic, butter, lemon juice, and salt.
3. Brush chicken pieces with spice mixture.
4. Place onion slices in bottom of broiler pan. Set chicken pieces on top. Add water to moisten pan.
5. Roast for about 1 hour or until chicken's internal temperature is 175°F (80°C). Baste occasionally.

14

Loyal Gizmos

For someone who grew up in a place called Nick's Coffee Counter, it might surprise you to learn that I didn't develop a taste for java until my late twenties. As a kid, I served tens of thousands of cups for ten cents each at my parents' lunch counter in Saint John, but always preferred to drink Coca-Cola. Profits from coffee sales might have paid my way to college (as my father maintained), but the ravages of all those bottles of Coke covered tuition for our dentist's kids.

By the mid-1970s, I was back in Saint John sharing an apartment with Colette, who had recently moved from Montréal to work at the local National Film Board office. Her boss was my pal, Wally, and he knew I could use help with the rent as badly as she needed accommodation. We were living next door to my high school friend, Bob. I was quick to make a pot of tea for friends in those days, but I still wasn't drinking coffee. Colette and Bob, however, *needed* their coffee—and not the instant kind, which I kept on hand for visitors. My friend Heather also noted this blind spot in my hospitality and guided me towards more civilized fare by giving me a Melitta kit: a tin of ground coffee, plastic cone, and paper filters. I loved the coffee it made. I abandoned tea.

But Colette and Bob wanted to accelerate my evolution. In a gesture of kindness (and naked self-interest), they gave me a Braun KSM 1 Coffee Grinder. This was in 1975, and, amazingly, I still use the same burnt-orange Braun every morning. In both design and function, it's no muss, no fuss. I press the white button, the motor whirrs, and the blades reduce coffee beans to powder. The longevity of this little gizmo fills me with wonder every time I set eyes on it. Why hasn't it broken down or worn out like every other electrical/mechanical device I've owned, from watches and radios to washing machines and cars? It's outlasted relationships, governments, and video stores.

I've fantasized about writing a fawning testimonial and sending it to Braun. Their marketing department would consider this a priceless gift, feature my steadfast grinder in an ad campaign touting the reliability of Braun products, use a pithy, heartwarming quote from me (*In a world of ugly, disposable objects...*), and then, in gratitude, send me gift certificates for a lifetime supply of their current devices. Which, if actuarial tables used by the insurance industry are accurate, won't have to last as long as my coffee grinder.

The Braun also performed double duty for a while, grinding spices—from coarse to fine—with ease. Unfortunately, even the most fastidious cleaning won't remove all the particles of a sharp Jamaican Curry or Creole Spice Blend from the next few batches of coffee (remnants of Lebanese Seven Spice blend, however, are always welcome in the morning brew). So I'm more likely to use the mortar and pestle or a new electric grinder for spices these days, and add the pinch of "L-7" separately. (TIP: To clean residue from your last episode of spice-grinding, buzz up 1 tablespoon of rice. The rice has enough abrasive strength to dislodge those bits of chili and turmeric, and after you brush it out, it leaves a more neutral environment.)

It's tempting to write a series of pieces on favourite kitchenware—like my grinder—that I've used for decades. There's the carved wooden spoon I bought in Cape Breton in the 1970s, the classic tin nutmeg grater (also ideal for tonka beans), the comically oversized garlic press that can smash six cloves at once,

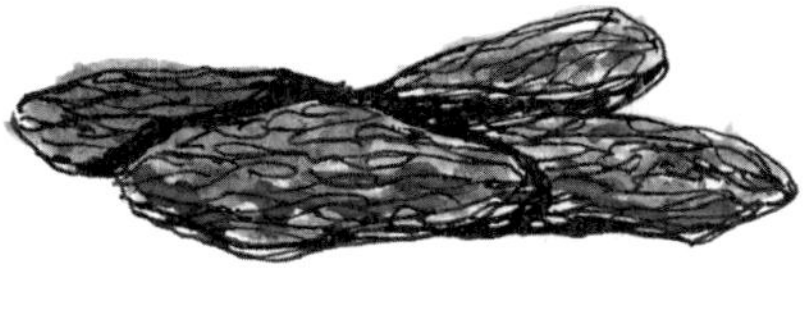

tonka beans

the slim Victorinox paring knife stationed beside the kitchen sink, etc. At some point in history, the ancestors of these common devices were technological breakthroughs. In our kitchens, we build sentimental attachments to them. And as McLuhan pointed out, "attachment" is just one step away from what they are: extensions of human body parts that pound like fists and cut like teeth.

In the meantime, visits from Colette, Bob, and Heather are long overdue. They need to monitor my progress towards becoming civilized. And the next time they come over, I know exactly what I'll serve.

Mesta Village Pasta

Serves 6

Dionysios' Wild Herb Blend, Pasilla de Oaxaca Flakes

What's better than a hearty dish you can serve up to friends in a single big bowl? This dish proves that the key to real gastronomy is a combination of simplicity and great basic ingredients. Dionysios' Wild Herb Blend is from the island of Chios, Greece, which is where Philippe and Ethné de Vienne first encountered this dish, in the village of Mesta.

To keep the meal authentically Greek, go for dry red wines such as Apelia, Okto by the Lyrarakis Winery in Crete, or Boutari's Naoussa. (Unfortunately, provincial liquor stores blow hot and cold on keeping Greek wines; good luck finding them.) The Pasilla de Oaxaca Flakes are not authentically Greek, of course—they're from Mexico—but they add a delightfully subtle heat to the complex flavours at play.

1 pound short pasta (such as penne, rotini, or ziti)
½ cup olive oil
½ cup pine nuts
¾ cup dried currants
6 garlic cloves, sliced
1 tablespoon Dionysios' Wild Herb Blend
5 cured anchovies, chopped finely
2 cups grape tomatoes, halved
1 teaspoon Pasilla de Oaxaca Flakes
¼ pound Greek *kefalotiri* (a hard, sharp, sheep's milk cheese, suitable for grating) or Romano cheese

1. Chop anchovies finely. Halve the tomatoes.
2. Cook pasta in salted, boiling water.
3. Heat oil in frying pan on medium heat. Brown pine nuts for 1 minute and remove with slotted spoon.
4. Fry currants until they puff up, about 1 minute, and remove.
5. Next, add sliced garlic to oil. Once golden, add Dionysios' Wild Herb Blend and anchovies. Cook for 1 minute.
6. Add halved tomatoes. Return pine nuts and currants to frying pan. Cook for 2 minutes, then add Pasilla de Oaxaca Flakes.
7. Drain pasta, reserving 1 cup of cooking water. Pour pasta into large bowl. Combine contents of frying pan with ½ cup of pasta water. Toss well.
8. Wait 1 minute before drizzling more oil and adding ½ the grated cheese. Toss pasta again. Add additional pasta water if dish is too dry.
9. Serve garnished with additional Pasilla de Oaxaca Flakes and remaining cheese.

15

Nothing Happened Here

I've watched enough gangster movies to say with authority that it's much easier to remove a body and clean up a blood-splattered murder scene than it is to get a Christmas tree out of the house and return the living room to its normal state. And despite all the sweeping and vacuuming, you know that one sunny morning in August, a fir, spruce, or pine needle (they're all equally treacherous) will crawl out from under the quarter-round and, in an act of cold revenge (*You shoulda watered me on New Year's Eve, you schmuck!*), lodge itself in the most tender part of your foot.

But what got me into this fix, anyway?

Like inviting an unsuspecting mobster into a set-up for a hit, the introduction of a six-foot-tall tree into a small living room appears innocent enough, but requires meticulous planning and luck.

The tree itself had been languishing outside since I brought it home from the lot about a week earlier. I was waiting for the seasonal sweet spot. This occurs sometime after *Why did you bring that tree into the house so soon—it'll be a fire hazard by Boxing Day!* and before *Isn't that tree up yet?* Ever the optimist, I had also been vainly hoping for ideal meteorological conditions to materialize. These would include (a) no recent snow or rain, and (b) temperatures slightly above the freezing point. Otherwise, when you lug in the tree, you risk irrigating the living room floor like so much parched farmland. Of course, hoping for "ideal conditions" for anything in the Maritimes probably defines the word "futile." It rained. It froze. It snowed.

Meanwhile, the annual migration of the furniture had begun. First, the heavy upholstered chair that presides over the living room like a fearsome dowager had to be moved to make space for the tree. To make space for the chair, I had to exile a side table to another room where it would stand until early in the New Year, shouting *I don't belong here!* to everyone. But even before transferring the side table to its temporary home, I had to carry the year's worth of books I had piled onto it to the basement. Then, with the help of an accomplice, we wrestled an end table that would be displaced by the tree to my daughter's room, where it might become part of the, uh, décor, until she concealed it with layers of clothing. And so on.

Enter the tree, depositing about a litre of runoff water.

Returning the house to its pre-Christmas condition also yielded disturbing surprises. Every December, we buy half a box of Florida oranges to support a local swim team's fundraiser and store it in plain sight on the dining-room floor. The risk of scurvy in the household plummets as we juice a few every morning. But in preparing for the seasonally adjusted population spike (returning children, their friends, family, neighbourhood celebrants), our "visitors" from the Sunshine State had to be "disappeared." While hunting for the treetop angel's box around January 6, I started excavating the laundry closet and found five oranges, which looked as if they had started to juice themselves into their cardboard box. Not pretty. But two weeks in a warm, dark closet will make you do strange things.

Now that the tree is back in the great outdoors, waiting for its drive to the chipper, and sleeper cells of fallen needles have escaped to plot assassination attempts on my feet later this year, the living room has started to look like nothing happened here. Except that it's The Day Before Market again. Nine boxes filled with spices. Two heavy-duty plastic containers jammed with display materials. Three accordion files exploding with recipes. The dining-room table and the living-room floor have taken on the look that's bound to be all the rage in interior design magazines this year: Warehouse Chic. With enough cardboard boxes and heavy-duty Rubbermaid plastic crates, you can have it, too. But by Saturday night, there won't be a trace of all this domestic mayhem.

Tony Soprano would be proud.

Warm Goat Cheese and Tomato Meze

Dionysios' Wild Herb Blend or Za'atar, and Isot Kurdish Black Pepper

Serves 6

Some people seem to have a great capacity for elaborate entertaining, even several times in the same season. But if you don't have that kind of social stamina and simply want to whip up something tasty in a hurry when company's coming, it's comforting to have a few recipes like the following in your repertoire. Use one of the following herb blends (or your own favourite), and garnish with a flaked or powdered pepper that has both mild heat and a fruity flavour.

Dionysios' Wild Herb Blend is an assortment of intensely aromatic and flavourful mountain herbs (marjoram, oregano, thyme) from the island of Chios, Greece. This aromatic mixture works beautifully in many dishes, including tomato sauces, fish, and Mediterranean appetizers.

An alternative is Za'atar, a classic Middle Eastern herb blend, which includes—and takes its name from—za'atar thyme (a seed that tastes like thyme), oregano, anise, fennel, cumin, toasted sesame seeds, sumac, and salt. While Isot (*EE-sot*) Kurdish Black Pepper (sun-dried black chili, flaked, and preserved with oil and salt) adds a rich fragrance with flavours that hint of raisin and tobacco.

This dish features goat cheese and grape tomatoes. It makes a quick, delicious appetizer on its own or with other mezes.

1 log goat cheese *or* feta
1 garlic clove, thinly sliced
12 grape tomatoes
¼ cup olive oil
pinch Dionysios' Wild Herb Blend *or* of Za'atar, and of Isot Kurdish Black Pepper on each
freshly ground black pepper

1. Preheat oven to 350°F (175°C).
2. Cut goat cheese into ½-inch slices and place in small ovenproof dish. Add thin slice garlic and 1 grape tomato to each.
3. Drizzle olive oil and sprinkle herbs and pepper.
4. Cook 13–15 minutes, until cheese is hot.
5. Serve with pita or pieces torn from a baguette or rustic loaf.

16

Fishbones and Fine Writing

In the late innings of a long winter, it's always a consolation to remember that in just a matter of weeks, shad will migrate up the Eastern Seaboard into the Bay of Fundy, then rocket past fiddleheads poking through the muddy margins of Maritime rivers to find the ideal place to spawn.

The flesh of a shad is delicate, white, fading to grey in places, with a slight sweetness. It also makes for a risky meal. Never eat shad in dim light or big bites. Three sets of bones (including a barbed set whose stragglers seem designed to lodge in your throat) make shad the least popular fish on your local seafood counter—if it shows up there at all. But for anyone who eats with the seasons, its arrival, elegantly synchronized with the fiddlehead harvest, is the true marker of spring in the Maritimes. Having a plate of baked shad and the dark, coiled fern in front of you can make you feel like royalty.

While waiting for shad, I've been doing the next best thing over the past few months: reading about it (appropriately, in small morsels). It's not that I'm obsessed with shad, but I love good writing, and *The Founding Fish* by John McPhee is a feast. It includes passages on the unique biology and quirky behaviour of shad. It exposes you to fierce historical debate (did the arrival of the spring run of shad save Washington's army from starvation and defeat in the American Revolutionary War, thus making it *The Founding Fish*?). It's populated by colourful characters (Armand Charest, who created a Rube Goldberg machine with tricycle wheels and bicycle chains so he and his wife could mass-produce shad darts for anglers without leaving their couch). And there are McPhee's confessions and deft observations from his experiences fishing for shad (out in his waders and up to his waist on the flooded banks of a river in spring, he writes that the rushing water just beyond him is *concentrated in a silt-laden flume of what appears to be hurtling cement*).

Chapter 6 of *The Founding Fish* focuses on the Maritimes' significance in the life of shad—the attractiveness of the Bay of Fundy to the species, the design of brush weirs in the Minas Basin, the research of Mike Dadswell at Acadia University, and the shad's second-fiddle relationship to the Atlantic salmon among anglers on the Miramichi. McPhee ends the book with recipes for shad and its roe, writing, *Ever since I learned how they cook whole shad in the Maritime Provinces of Canada, I have seldom done it another way.*

Like all good non-fiction writers, McPhee delivers truckloads of facts without ever making you feel he's dumping his research on you. Of the movement of baby shad heading from their freshwater birthplace towards the ocean in autumn, he describes a phenomenon known as "dimpling":

> *They are coming down the river in galactic schools, and at dusk especially they will turn the water white. They dimple, dapple, leap into the air. They seem like a squall of silver rain.... What the human eye sees, as it observes the dimpling of the shad on the blue river bordered with turning leaves, is early Impressionism...*

Even though he's a shad aficionado, McPhee is, above all, a writer. He's tackled subjects from the Swiss Army to long-haul freight carriers and modern cattle rustling, all with equal verve, and most often in *The New Yorker*. For every ten thousand hacks churning out pieces on sports or politics or film, there is one writer who manages to turn a reader previously uninterested in the topic at hand into an eager page-turner. And until the lusty shad show up for their northern version of an uninhibited Spring Break and one of them finds its way into my kitchen, you can find me turning the pages of *The Founding Fish*. Eagerly.

Where To Find Shad

If you're not an angler (I'm not), you can get shad in one of two places: off the back of a truck or at a seafood counter. If it's at the latter, take advantage of a fishmonger's skills and equipment by getting him or her to scale the fish. If there are any scales left when you handle the fish at home, don't put them down the drain—they're as hard as guitar picks and could become the basis of a plumbing emergency. Then decide whether you want the whole shad (to bake) or fillets—either boned or unboned. If you want to bake the fish, ask the fishmonger to remove the head, fins and tail (and those pesky scales).

John McPhee is a thorough writer, so it shouldn't be a surprise that he included an appendix to *The Founding Fish*, which contains recipes. He alerts us to the peculiar stages that shad flesh transits as it cooks. For unboned fillets, McPhee writes, *As shad muscle broils, it will soften before it sets. After eleven or twelve minutes, it will almost be soup. After fifteen and a half minutes, it is firm and just done. Past sixteen, it is overdone.* Throw in the variability of oven temperatures, and you get an idea of how vigilant you have to be while cooking shad.

As for boned fillets, McPhee points out that the shad's adipose tissue provides a self-basting "nutty butter." All that's needed is something to complement the fattiness—lemon or a mixture of two parts soy sauce to one part sesame oil, with either chopped scallions or minced ginger. He puts on some before he slides the fillets under the broiler and a little when he removes them.

Now—my favourite: whole, baked shad. McPhee is categorical. As I've mentioned, he states that he hasn't found a better way than the method he learned in the Maritimes.

McPhee says, *Salt and pepper the skin and the empty cavity. Pack it up with turkey stuffing until the filled gap between the belly flaps is something like two inches. During the thirty-five baking minutes, you don't need to roll the fish over.*

When serving, McPhee advises that you *cant* [tilt] *it upward, more or less on its back, and open it as you would a trout.* This makes it easier to lift out the backbone and ribs. There will still be bones because, well, it's a shad. I would recommend that you enjoy this quintessential Maritime spring delicacy under the glare of an unromantic, unfrosted one hundred-watt light bulb.

Spiced Braised Rhubarb

Green Indian Cardamom, Star Anise, Vanilla Bean, Ginger

Makes 6 servings (or more if used as a topping on ice cream or yoghurt)

Another edible harbinger of spring is rhubarb. Welcome the season with this delicious fruit compote. While the orange juice and honey tenderize the tart rhubarb, the aromatic green cardamom, star anise, and vanilla flavour the intense syrup.

1½ pounds rhubarb stalks, trimmed and cut into 2-inch pieces on an angle (like penne)
1 cup fresh orange juice
¼ cup honey
½ teaspoon kosher salt
8 green cardamom pods
2 star anise
1 vanilla bean, split lengthwise, seeds scraped and reserved
1 (1½-inch) piece ginger, peeled and thickly sliced, crosswise
yoghurt or vanilla ice cream, to serve

1. Heat oven to 400°F (200°C)
2. Mix together rhubarb, orange juice, honey, salt, green cardamom, star anise, vanilla bean (and seeds), and ginger in a 9 × 13-inch baking dish.
3. Bake, stirring occasionally, until rhubarb is tender (14–16 minutes).
4. Let cool to room temperature, then serve over yoghurt or ice cream, if you like.

~ 17 ~

Winners and Losers

Underdog. Wallflower. Always the bridesmaid, never the bride. Our language is rich in words and phrases to describe people who fail to end up on the right side of the popularity/success/celebrity line.

And the way we react to the "also-rans" and "second fiddles" of the world often says a lot about us. Are we reflexively sympathetic? Or do we give these unfortunates a wide berth, for fear of...what? That their lack of success would rub off on us? Hmm. Let's leave that to the psychologists. But not yet. Perhaps this aversion towards "losers" is the flip side of why so many people are addicted to celebrity culture. And where addiction reigns, there are huge profits to be made.

In February of 2012, a young NBA player named Jeremy Lin became a starter with the New York Knicks. He had some surprisingly good games, and within a week, licensed "Lin" basketball jerseys, posters, and related gear were flying off the shelves. Sales at the Knicks's online store shot up 4,000 per cent, and the whole world of sports retailing enjoyed a mid-winter revenue bump. Meanwhile, nobody was even manufacturing jerseys that carried the name of the perfectly competent, professional athlete at the end of the bench who only got called into the game when the team had a fat lead in the last few minutes of play.

But whenever you buy stuff that you hope will identify you with celebrity success, you've just made a shaky investment. (And who designs the rap stars' "designer" perfume and the actors' "designer" clothing lines, anyway?) Commemorative teacups for Chuck and Di's storybook wedding? Lance

Armstrong cycling gear? The flash flood of outrage that follows indiscretions can wash away carefully manicured images and fragile loyalties in a day.

As you've probably guessed, my default position is to root for underdogs, or at least try to get other people to give more serious consideration to their good, but overshadowed, qualities. For instance, in the days when 45 rpm recordings had a heavily promoted "A" side and some musical afterthought on the "B," nothing gave me more of a kick than to find a tune on "the flip side" that a fellow music fan would find more interesting than the "hit." Ditto for great films that don't come surfing into town like the vacuous blockbusters on their multimillion-dollar waves of promotion.

And for some mysterious reason, that attitude is still with me. Since I started my very small business as a spice merchant, I'm always pleased to see lesser-known products climbing up the spice charts. This is largely due to word-of-mouth from customers who've dared to take a chance on a blend that doesn't have a "brand." Who would have thought that Ethiopian Berberé sales would eclipse those of Madras Curry? Not I. So what would make you invite a wallflower spice blend to dance in your kitchen? How about a few recipes?

Using familiar ingredients as a base is always an excellent way to acquaint yourself with the flavour of an unfamiliar blend of spices. And while you're enjoying an old favourite (scrambled eggs, haddock) that's been perked up by a new-to-you spice combination, think of what else the blend might enhance.

Spicy Cheese Bites

Any spice blend you've never tried

MAKES ABOUT 2 DOZEN

These savoury cheese bites are easy and delicious—just the thing to whip up if you have friends in for an evening of board games in the winter, or out in the yard for a few cold ones on a summer afternoon.

½ pound butter, room temperature
1 cup sharp cheddar cheese (at least 2 years old), grated
2 cups flour
½ cup Rice Krispies
2 teaspoons any spice blend, ground (Jamaican Curry, Chai Spice Blend, Chinese Five Spices, Spice Coast Garam Masala, etc.)

1. Cream butter and cheese together.
2. Gradually add other ingredients and mix until smooth.
3. Roll into small balls and place on cookie sheet. Press down with fork.
4. Bake at 350°F (180°C) for 30 minutes.

Spiced Mayonnaise

Any spice blend

MAKES 1¼ CUPS

Mayonnaise is another perfect backdrop for spices. Use it as a dip for vegetables or frites, and a condiment for anything from sausages to fish cakes.

2 egg yolks
2 tablespoons lemon juice
1 teaspoon any spice blend, ground
A few grinds fresh pepper
pinch salt
1 cup extra-virgin olive oil

1. Make sure all ingredients are at room temperature.
2. Whisk egg yolks until they become thick and resistant.
3. Whisk in lemon juice, ground spices, pepper, and salt.
4. Start whisking in oil—at first, drop by drop. When mayonnaise starts to thicken, increase addition of oil to a thin, steady stream—but keep whisking.
5. To thin mayonnaise, whisk in more lemon juice or hot water.
6. Store, covered, in fridge for up to 3 days.

Spiced Quinoa

Serves 4 (or more as a side dish at a potluck)

Wholesome Curry, Black Pepper, Cinnamon

This recipe features power foods quinoa and chickpeas, combining pungent Mediterranean and Indian flavours for a quick and delicious side dish. Wholesome Curry is a mild blend of spices, all of which have antioxidant properties: turmeric, coriander, black pepper, ginger, fennel, clove, mace, thyme, paprika, and cardamom.

1 tablespoon olive oil
1 small onion, chopped
1 clove garlic, minced
¾ cup quinoa
1½ teaspoons Wholesome Curry, ground (or any ground spice blend)
½ teaspoon freshly ground black pepper
¼ teaspoon cinnamon
1½ cups chicken stock
1 can chickpeas (*or less*), drained and rinsed
½ cup toasted pine nuts
Optional: ½ cup currants, or to taste

1. Stir together olive oil, onion, and garlic in a saucepan over medium heat until onion is soft and translucent.
2. Stir in quinoa, all spices and seasonings, and chicken stock. Bring to a boil, then reduce heat to medium-low. Cover and simmer until quinoa is tender and most of the liquid is absorbed (20–25 minutes).
3. Stir in drained chickpeas, toasted pine nuts, and currants.
4. Serve warm or cold.

18

Ducks, Thunderbirds, and Grains of Paradise

When choosing a car, would you rather buy one called a "Duck" or a "Thunderbird"?

The first time you're invited to your fiancé's parents' place for dinner, which wine is more likely to create a better impression: Fat Bastard or Châteauneuf-du-Pape?

Which is the better quality ice cream: Aunt Gertrude's or Häagen-Dazs?

Branding, marketing, and advertising are braided as tightly as a sailor's knot. And while pros can disentangle them, is doesn't really matter which strand turns out to be most important in the selling of a product or idea. Ultimately, success will depend on making smart choices all along the way and avoiding terrible ones.

That's why no automobile manufacturer will ever try to foist a car called a "Duck" on consumers. Fat Bastard is a great name if you're trying to sell wine to a twenty-something guy headed to a potluck at his pals' apartment. The marketing team, however, will not take responsibility if the same dude creates a social disaster by taking it to the potential in-laws' place. And while Aunt Gertrude might make the most delicious ice cream ever created, Reuben Mattus won domination of the super-premium market when he dreamed up the ridiculous, vaguely Scandinavian-looking Häagen-Dazs for his higher butterfat, less airy dairy product.

This kind of thing has been going on for longer than you might imagine. Take, for example, *amomum meligueta*, which grows in the vicinity of modern-day Liberia and Sierra Leone as well as parts of the Caribbean. Through the centuries, it has also been known as guinea pepper, alligator pepper, and ginny grains. It was already showing up in the thirteenth-century records of Emperor John III's court physician, though under its most successful name: *grana paradisi*, or Grains of Paradise.

In those days, it was carried overland from West Africa to what is now Libya, where it was bought by Venetian traders and shipped to markets in Italy and France. This transit route ensured that Grains of Paradise became part of the spicing in North African dishes. And yes, the grains still appear in Tajine Spices and Ras-el-hanout (variously translated as "top of the shelf" or "roof of the shop"—the signature blend unique to each spice merchant). The Italian traders had no idea where the tiny seeds originated—they just knew they had a wonderful taste: a combination of pepper, cardamom, coriander, ginger, and citrus. So they had started calling them "Grains of Paradise." *Yeah, that's it,* you can just hear some clever Venetian trader saying, *I'll tell them that these come from the Garden of Eden!*

A century later, European ships sailed directly to the west coast of Africa, and the products they acquired there led to the naming of several colonies: Gold Coast, Ivory Coast, and...Grain Coast. Tragically, the trade in humans would also yield the name "Slave Coast" to this part of the continent.

In 1470 Portugal declared a monopoly on the highly valued Grains of Paradise from the West African coast (along with precious gems and "unicorns," which were actually rhinoceros horns). The English developed a taste for the

grains in *hippocras*, a spiced wine. Reportedly, Elizabeth I enjoyed Grains of Paradise in her wine and ale, but later, on one of his "mad" days, King George III would declare this spicy additive illegal, with fines for any brewer who used it or for any apothecary who sold it to him.

HELLO ALL YOU ANTI-ESTABLISHMENT MICROBREWERS OUT THERE, FIGHT THE MAN: SPIKE YOUR ALE WITH GRAINS OF PARADISE!

Now, back to our essay.

The expansion of the European spice trade to India and even further east eventually brought back huge volumes of black peppercorns, which surpassed the guinea pepper/Grains of Paradise in popularity. By the end of the 1400s, the once-fabled grains were used as ballast in the ships that used to carry them as valuable cargo.

I've seen Grains of Paradise described in contemporary books as becoming "an irrelevance" and "almost unprocurable." Thanks to the efforts of my Spice Trekker buddies, Philippe and Ethné de Vienne, I procured some. Despite that coup, sales were unspectacular, mainly because I didn't have any recipes that called for the insignificant-looking, but tasty, grains.

One week, though, I decided they were just too darned special not to be part of the spicing options in more kitchens. So I resolved to find a few recipes that would let Grains of Paradise shine. In a spot of luck, I'd been invited out to supper at Salty's, the Halifax-waterfront restaurant co-owned by my old pal and former college roommate, Brendan (yes, I know that the fact he was my roomie in college makes him old). What had we studied, you ask? Brendan studied engineering and became a successful restaurateur. I studied physics and ended up in broadcast journalism for thirty-plus years. Remember this, kids, whenever adults start nattering about the importance of studying something that will lead directly to a job after graduation.

Anyway, Brendan kindly indulged me and asked his bartender to test a cocktail recipe I'd brought, which featured Grains of Paradise. It was called "Bloody Paradise." We all thought the amount of balsamic vinegar in the ingredients ("1 tablespoon") seemed excessive. Surely "1 tsp" was intended. His bartender made both versions. The "straw poll" (*sip, sip*) was unanimous: the 1-tablespoon version would stand—and even with the amount of balsamic called for, the Grains held their own and added a citric, peppery kick.

But my luck got even better. West African Peanut Soup was on the menu. Surely a spice that originated in that part of the world would complement it. It did, perfectly (even though my Grains of Paradise were cultivated in Trinidad). A fresh grind of Grains of Paradise on that rich, golden soup looked grand and tasted even better. Further research revealed that these grains can be used deliciously in salads, on grilled or fresh vegetables, in chocolate, and on sautéed scallops.

Try the recipes I just mentioned and decide whether the name is an early example of slick marketing or the poetic acknowledgement of a very special spice.

Bloody Paradise

Grains of Paradise

MAKES 1 DRINK

The guinea pepper might not have originated in the Garden of Eden, but it adds a unique tingle to this cocktail—an earthly delight on a hot day. The vodka from Lunenburg, Nova Scotia's Ironworks Distillery is made with Annapolis Valley apples, instead of the more traditional potatoes or grain.

¼ teaspoon salt (or to taste)
½ teaspoon coarsely ground Grains of Paradise
1 cup tomato juice
2 tablespoons lime juice
1 tablespoon balsamic vinegar
1½ ounces Ironworks Distillery vodka

Garnish
Grains of Paradise to taste
2 basil leaves, fried in oil and sprinkled with salt

1. In a shaker, mix all ingredients. Shake well.
2. Pour over a glass of ice. Grind more Grains of Paradise over drink, and garnish with basil leaves.

West African Peanut and Sweet Potato Stew

Grains of Paradise

Serves 6

For a spice that was once a huge fad in Europe, Grains of Paradise/guinea pepper fell out of favour for centuries. This particular recipe can trace its origins to the groundnut stews of Sierra Leone. Guinea pepper, which is related to cardamom and ginger, adds the perfect accent to any liquid you sip—like soup or a tomato juice-based cocktail.

2 sweet potatoes, peeled and cubed
3 garlic cloves, minced
3 tablespoons grated fresh ginger root
2 tablespoons ground coriander
½ teaspoon ground cayenne (or to taste)
2 tablespoons vegetable oil
4 cups chopped onion
2 tomatoes, chopped
4 cups eggplant, peeled and cubed
½ cup vegetable stock *or* water
1 cup chopped zucchini *or* yellow summer squash
2 green peppers, coarsely chopped
2 cups tomato juice
½ cup peanut butter
freshly ground Grains of Paradise to taste

1 Steam or boil sweet potato cubes until just tender.

2 Meanwhile, sauté garlic, ginger root, and spices in vegetable oil for one minute.

3 Add onions. Cook until they begin to soften.

4 Add tomatoes, eggplant, and vegetable stock. Simmer for 10 minutes.

5 Add zucchini and green peppers. Simmer until all vegetables are tender, about 20 minutes

6 Drain sweet potatoes and add to stew along with tomato juice and peanut butter. Stir well.

7 Simmer on very low heat for 5 to 10 minutes. Stir occasionally to prevent sticking.

8 Serve on rice or Couscous (see p. 52).

9 Grind fresh Grains of Paradise over each serving.

19

Scheherazade or the Saint

In the Catholic tradition, there's a patron saint for every trade. Journalism is no exception.

St. Frances de Sales got the nod from the Vatican in 1923, a time when—in the journalistic tradition—a reporter kept a lit stogie in one side of his mouth, profanities spouting from the other, and a flask of whiskey stashed in the roll-top desk. The mortal sin of hacking cellphones for scoops hadn't even been imagined yet, but when it was, it must have been comforting to know there was a saint on heavenly speed-dial who could guide even Rupert Murdoch's ink-stained wretches back to the path of righteousness. But I think there's a more appropriate figure for journalists to revere—someone for whom the word "deadline" had a literal edge.

According to legend, a Persian shah whose wife had been unfaithful devised a plan to prevent this from ever happening again. He would marry a virgin, and after relieving her of this designation on their wedding night, he would send her off to the executioner in the morning (perhaps the source of the phrase "Queen For A Day"...). After dispatching 1,000 young women in this way, it didn't require Wikileaks for word to get around the kingdom that the shah was a bad date. Despite this, an exceptionally well-read and gifted storyteller by the name of Scheherazade offered herself up as bride number 1,001.

So with the ultimate looming deadline, Scheherazade did what all good journalists do: stalled for time. She persuaded the shah to let her tell her sister a final story (don't ask me why her sister was hanging out in the bedroom on the wedding night—the shah's household wasn't exactly emblematic of family values). Scheherazade's story must have had a great hook and a gripping narrative, because the shah was entranced. Cleverly, she spun it out until sunrise—the customary deadline for the executioner to edit heads from bodies—without concluding the story. Despite the shah's pleading that she tie up the loose ends, Scheherazade persuaded him to let her do so the following night. (Journalists will recognize this as the moment you persuade a producer or editor you have so much good material that it should be expanded into a series.)

Every night, Scheherazade would conclude the previous story and start a new one, which—gee whiz—would be interrupted by the rising sun. "Ali Baba and the Forty Thieves," "The Voyages of Sinbad," "Aladdin's Lamp," you name it—the shah grudgingly accepted the to-be-continued ploy. When Scheherazade finished her one thousandth tale, she told him she had no more stories to tell, but by this time her masterful storytelling had apparently mellowed the bloody-minded shah. After all those short-term contract queens, he gave Scheherazade the staff position, with benefits and a no-termination clause.

With all due respect to St. Francis de Sales, I would nominate Scheherazade as an infinitely more appropriate inspiration for journalists and writers of all varieties.

Thousand-and-One-Nights Chicken

Thousand and One Nights Blend

SERVES 4

Thousand and One Nights blend is Philippe de Vienne's version of a classic of Middle East medieval cuisine: black pepper, sumac (a reddish-purple, powdered bush berry with a lemony tartness), cumin, mint, turmeric, ginger, coriander, cardamom, allspice, cinnamon, rosebuds, rose petals, kentjur (a rhizome similar to ginger), mastic, bay leaves, galangal (another rhizome, common in Thai and Indonesian cuisine), and clove.

The first time I offered it for sale, I was happy to discover that the blend caught the attention of writer Valerie Compton, author of *Tide Road* (a fine novel nominated for the 2012 Thomas Head Raddall Atlantic Fiction Award). Valerie soon returned for more tins. I couldn't imagine she was using that much herself. I asked if she'd be so kind as to share the explanation, and she did:

Okay, so I bought it for the name.

But when I opened the tin, I was captivated by its looks. So many spices I didn't recognize! And nestled amongst them: one perfect, whole rosebud. It took me days to work up the emotional distance necessary to grind all that beauty into a usable powder. When I finally did, I was transported to medieval Persia by a fragrance like nothing I'd inhaled before. What was it made of? I went on a research quest—and what symbolic sticking power I found. The rosebuds, so sweet-looking, were bitter. There was sourness, courtesy of the sumac and galangal. Warmth from cumin and black pepper. And what was mastic? In his fascinating and exhaustive Penguin Companion to Food, Alan Davidson explains that mastic is "tears" of resin secreted by the stems of a shrub in the pistachio family when it is wounded. It's a taste that was common in medieval Islamic cookery.

I've been giving tins of the Thousand and One Nights blend to my women writer friends, hoping it will work for them like a magic potion. I warn them that this concoction needs rich, dark meat, and coddling over a low flame to reach its delicious potential. I think they get the idea: there's time for stories while you wait.

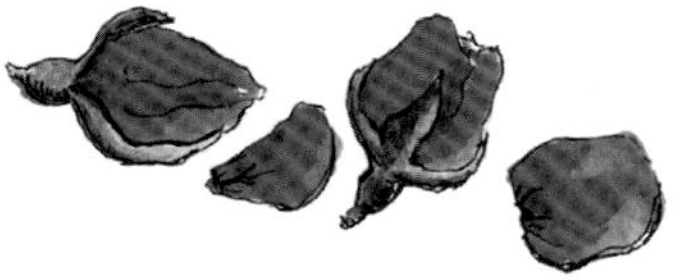

rosebuds

The fact that Valerie has been fuelling the imaginations of writers across Canada with gifts of this blend delights me to no end. And sharing stories while the meal simmers is even better. (Because sharing good stories keeps you alive—right, Scheherazade?)

The recipe itself is a culinary heirloom from tenth-century Baghdad. The scribe of *Kitab al-Tabikh* ("The Book of Dishes") mined recipes from centuries-old personal collections of caliphs and aristocrats. The original version of this simple but wonderfully spiced chicken dish recommends truffles, but if your pantry is like mine (what? Out of truffles again?), Philippe suggests using carrots or squash.

1 (3–4 pound) chicken, cut into pieces
1½ tablespoons ground Thousand and One Nights blend
¼ cup olive oil
3 onions, quartered
3 cloves garlic
2 cups carrot sticks *or* vegetable of choice
2 cups chickpeas, cooked
salt to taste
pita bread to cover bottom of serving dish
1 lemon, quartered, for garnish

1. Remove skin and excess fat from chicken pieces.
2. Season chicken with ground Thousand and One Nights blend.
3. Heat olive oil and cook onions, garlic, and chicken together. Brown for 5 to 10 minutes over medium heat.
4. Add vegetables of choice, chickpeas and salt. Simmer for 30 minutes.
5. To serve, tear pita bread into pieces and place in bottom of shallow serving dish. Pour ragout over bread. Garnish with herbs and lemon quarters.

20

Fear, Cooking, and the Grill

New technologies erase older technologies from our lives without a single teardrop of sentimentality. This applies as much to cooking devices as it does to horse-drawn carriages or cassettes.

When I was growing up, I remember overhearing my mother and her friends trading horrific stories of pressure cookers and gas stoves exploding. This was the decade that segued from the Second World War straight into the Cold War; explosions were never far from adults' minds. We didn't have a pressure cooker or a gas stove (the latter because natural gas never got further east than Montréal). But locally, there seemed to be a steady supply of third-hand tales of pressure cookers maiming or killing unfortunate domestic cooks with stainless steel shrapnel propelled by scalding, superheated steam. If food particles blocked the safety valve, the innocent device cooking the family supper transformed into a bomb.

Whether these events were happening as frequently as I heard about them, I don't know. Hearsay was eagerly accepted as fact. Despite the cheery retro advertisements we see of smiling housewives and dapper husbands of the 1950s, I recall the period as one laced with fear. There were vivid memories of husbands, brothers, and sons killed or mentally shattered in the recent war. This was sandwiched with the threat of imminent nuclear war (go to the CBC Archives site for a report by the legendary Norman DePoe, who interviews the McCallum family as they emerge from a week in a fallout shelter.) Just add McCarthy-era fear-mongering about Communist spies infiltrating every community, sprinkle with actual radioactive fallout from atomic-bomb tests, and *voilà*: people's dreams were shot through with nightmares.

Was the pressure cooker a casualty of that collective 1950s anxiety? Who knows? I'll leave that answer to a master's student in sociology. But once-common cooking devices come and go for any number of mysterious reasons.

Fast forward a few decades and we come to the transitional 1970s. Suddenly, everyone—especially baby boomers, who had finally fled the nest and settled into their first apartments—seemed to have that barbecue gizmo: the hibachi, complete with a heavy bag of charcoal briquettes and a range of dubious petroleum-based "starters." Cooking outdoors? It was liberating. Especially in a country where cold, miserable weather confines us to barracks for too much of the year.

The hibachis were usually made of cast iron, and left outdoors for the winter. This ensured that around season three, there would come a night when hot coals would tumble through the rusted bottom. If this happened on a wooden deck after you'd finished eating and moved inside for music and beer and other distractions, the next knock on the door was from the fire department (this happened to a friend in Saint John, you know who you are…).

To add to the hazards of the hibachi, small grates meant that cooking for more than about four people could be a long process. And if anyone got impatient and put the last burgers or chicken over cooling embers, indigestion was the least of your gastrointestinal worries.

But for all its limitations, the hibachi was the gateway to grilling for a whole generation. The marketing of larger, shinier, and more sophisticated barbecues pushed the humble hibachi into yard sales, if not extinction. It added *refill propane tank* to the list of common household chores. And it opened up a new world of culinary possibilities.

So remember, turn off the gas when you're finished cooking. You don't want to be the source of a cooking story that frightens the children.

Grilling Recipes and Tips

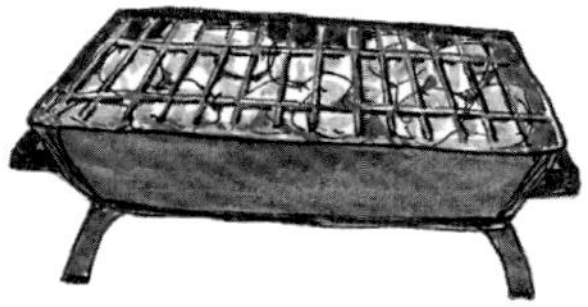

The taste of grilled food doesn't need anything fancy or expensive, as I was reminded on my 2012 trip to visit relatives in Greece. We dined on delicious lamb and pork chops, cooked on a grill that was supported by cinder blocks over wood embers tended on the ground.

These days, I'm happy to be an enabler of the grilling obsession. Meat, fish, vegetables—I've got spices and blends for all of 'em: Steak Rub, Satay Spices, Masala Grilling Spices, Oaxacan and Tlalelolco Rubs, and the BBQ Classic Blend with no sugar or salt). I also stock a Grilling Spice Kit with six different blends.

Don't forget curry blends (mild, wholesome, and Madras, among others). They tend to be overlooked as a part of barbecue preparations, which is a shame, because they make great marinades.

Marinating helps keep meat moist over the grill's intense heat, and the olive oil in the marinade transfers the flavour of spices into the meat without breaking down its texture.

BBQ Curry Marinade

Any curry blend,
Cilanto or Mint

MAKES ¾ CUP

½ cup olive oil
6 cloves minced garlic
1 teaspoon any curry blend
¼ cup minced fresh cilantro *or* mint
1 teaspoon salt
1 teaspoon freshly ground pepper

Simply whisk together.

Grilled Chicken Masala with Yoghurt Marinade

Masala Grill Blend,
Ginger

SERVES 4

The Masala Grill Blend brings together the aromas of Indian cuisine, for all kinds of grilled meats. It blends dehydrated onion, coriander, cumin, turmeric, dried ginger, garlic, black pepper, amchoor (dried, powdered unripe mango), lime, cardamom, cinnamon, mace, and clove. It's great for chicken, lamb, or pork.

Meat should marinate 24 hours to tenderize and flavour properly. And if the weather suddenly turns foul, you can roast your lovingly marinated chicken in the oven and put it under the broiler just before serving to crisp up the spicy crust. You'll love the succulent results and will be sure to add this technique to your grilling repertoire.

Indian Yoghurt Marinade

½ tablespoon ground Masala Grill Blend
6 garlic cloves
1 (1-inch) piece peeled fresh ginger
1 cup yoghurt
salt to taste

Put all ingredients in blender and process until smooth.

Grilled Chicken Masala

1 (3–4 pound) chicken
Indian Yoghurt Marinade (see above)
⅓ cup ghee or olive oil
Optional garnish: 2 teaspoons ground Spice Coast Garam Masala, sprinkled on top just before serving.

1 Cut chicken between breasts and flatten. Remove as much skin and fat as possible.
2 Slash meat deeply to allow marinade to penetrate. Rub marinade all over. Rest 24 hours in fridge.
3 Remove chicken from fridge 1 hour before cooking.
4 Brush chicken with ghee or vegetable oil. Roast in a 500°F (250°C) oven or on a hot grill.
5 Turn chicken over and baste regularly with more ghee or oil until cooked (15–20 minutes). Internal temperature of chicken should be 175°F (80°C). If cooking in oven, turn on broiler during last minutes to brown the spice crust.

Mexican-style Grilled Corn

Cajun or Chili Spices or Tlalelolco or Oaxacan Rub

SERVES 6 (AS A SIDE)

Pre-cooking unhusked corn in the microwave is fast and easy. It's also very easy to remove the husks and silk after this cooking method. Then grill quickly.

6 corn ears, unhusked

Grilling Paste
4 teaspoons butter *or* vegetable oil
2 teaspoons ground Cajun or Chili Spices, or Tlalelolco or Oaxacan Rub
¼ teaspoon salt

Optional Serving Sauce
¼ cup light mayonnaise
3 tablespoons sour cream
3 tablespoons minced fresh cilantro leaves
2 gloves garlic, minced
½ teaspoon ground spices or rub of your choice
¼ teaspoon ground black pepper
4 teaspoons juice from 1 lime
½ cup grated Parmesan or Romano cheese

Optional Serving Sauce

1 Combine mayonnaise, sour cream, cilantro, garlic, ground spices or rub, black pepper, lime juice, and cheese in large bowl; set aside.

Microwaved Corn

1 Combine butter, salt, and 2 teaspoons of spices or rub. Reserve.
2 Cook corn in microwave with husks and silk intact. Place dampened paper towel under corn. For 2 ears, cook 3–4 minutes; for 3 ears, 5–6 minutes; for 4 ears, 7–8 minutes; for 6 ears, 8–9 minutes.
3 At halfway point, turn ears over and rearrange.
4 When hot to the touch, remove from oven and wrap in towel or foil for 5 minutes.
5 Remove husks and silk.
6 Brush Grilling Paste on microwaved corn.
7 Grill corn on very hot, well-oiled grill, turning frequently until lightly charred all around.
8 Serve immediately as is, or with Optional Serving Sauce.

cumin

Classic Turkish Kebabs

Turkish Kebab Spice Blend

SERVES 4

The Turkish Kebab Spice Blend combines Aleppo pepper, Maraş pepper, cumin, oregano, and mint, for the authentic flavours of traditional Turkish cuisine. Use this blend to marinate meat for grilling or barbecuing—with or without skewers. It can also be used to season chicken or to marinate a piece of filet mignon. For vegetarian cuisine, add a pinch to chickpea stews.

Marinade

1 onion, grated
4 cloves garlic, chopped
4 teaspoons ground Turkish Kebab Spice Blend
2 tablespoons lemon juice
3 tablespoons olive oil

Kebabs

1 pound lamb, cubed (shoulder, leg, etc.)
1-pint box grape tomatoes *or* cherry tomatoes
2 bell peppers, cut into chunks
salt to taste

1. In a bowl, add grated onion to remaining Marinade ingredients and blend well.
2. Marinate lamb cubes for at least 1 hour (ideally up to 48 hours).
3. Skewer cubes of meat alternately with whole tomatoes and pepper chunks and grill over medium heat.
4. Salt, to taste, after cooking.
5. Serve with a fresh salad of greens, mint, and finely sliced cucumber strips in vinaigrette.

21

Proudly Amateur

Friday, late June.

One of the clichés of concert movies is the opening time-lapse sequence. It begins with an empty field. Then trailer trucks zap into the frame, roadies and technicians swarm around like caffeinated ants erecting the stage; metal frames shoot for the sky, clouds fly by, lights and supersized video screens are hung, banks of amplifiers are installed, shadows lengthen to mark the passage of the day, concertgoers flood the field, and *BANG!* With a flash of pyrotechnics, we're back in real time and familiar opening chords spark a roar of recognition from the crowd.

This is not happening in my backyard tonight....

What is happening—on a smaller scale, in my neighbour's backyard—is the set-up for his annual Tarp Party. It takes its name from the blue plastic tarp that protects what is essentially an outdoor kitchen party from being dampened by rain (it also helps contain the sound in a residential area). The party's formula is simple: family, friends, neighbours, potluck, and music. There is plenty of singing and playing—much of it in tune. In the years of the Tarp Party's existence, the police have only been summoned once: new neighbours were out of town, hadn't received word, returned home that night and complained about the unexpected noise. They've since become enthusiastic participants.

It always reminds me of an interesting point made by Annie Lennox, the charismatic lead singer of Eurythmics. She and her then-partner Dave Stewart exploded onto the scene just as music videos were becoming the centre of pop culture. It was all futuristic, androgynous outfits, neon hair, synthesizers, electronic beats, cool art direction, and slick production. You could only watch in awe. But years later, I saw a poignant interview with Lennox. She said she felt partly responsible for a sad development in music history: turning music lovers from participants into spectators. When she was growing up in Scotland, everyone sang or played instruments at house parties (it didn't even have to be a party—any gathering was reason enough to sing and play music). But Lennox went on to say that the over-the-top production values of the performers of her generation had made the simple act of music-making seem shabby by comparison. The perception was that if you couldn't replicate what you saw in a music video, you should keep your mouth shut and your guitar in its case.

Music is just one of the amateur joys we need to put back into everyday life. Lennox's reflections could also apply to what's happened to cooking. The superstar chefs, the impossibly complicated recipes with hard-to-source ingredients and intimidating preparations that sound like parodies of themselves (*care to whip up a pomegranate-achiote-sturgeon roe reduction, anyone?).* The act of cooking, like making music, is portrayed as something that should be handled exclusively by professionals. The message is "Do NOT try this at home."

The heck with that. Such thinking leads to reliance on microwaveable meals and takeout eaten in front of a TV screen without making eye contact with the person next to you. So tonight, instead of getting a good night's rest before tomorrow's early start for the market, I'll be next door with people who risk singing and playing instruments instead of playing Wii Rock Band, cooking instead of ordering out, and socializing face to face instead of online.

Just don't speak too loudly tomorrow morning.

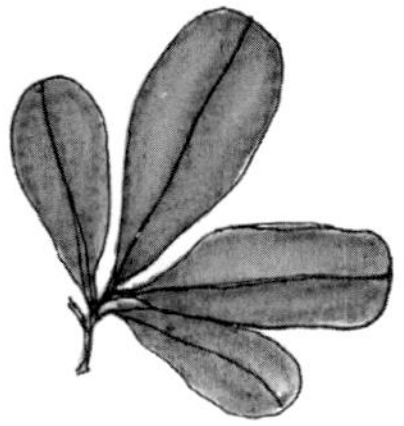

West Indian bay leaf

Jerk Chicken

Jerk Spices

SERVES 4

A plate of hot Jerk Chicken pieces is always welcome at a Tarp Party or potluck. It's believed that jerk spices were first made by Caribbean Indians in Jamaica. "Jerk" refers both to the indigenous spices in the blend (allspice, habanero chili, thyme, shallot, mace, and West Indian bay leaf) and the cooking technique. The pork was marinated with jerk spices for several hours, then slowly cooked or smoked—originally over a pit, then later in half of a fifty-five-gallon oil drum lined with coals, and later still, over a barbecue apparatus. Jerk spices can be used on all meats.

The Jerk Spices blend respects the tradition of the original recipe.

16 chicken drumsticks (skinless if preferred) *or* other chicken pieces
2 tablespoons vegetable oil
1 tablespoon ground Jerk Spices (2 if you really like heat)
Juice of 1 lime

1. Lightly coat chicken pieces with vegetable oil.
2. Generously coat chicken with ground Jerk Spices. Marinate several hours or overnight in refrigerator.
3. Place chicken in roasting pan, in a single layer. Sprinkle with lime juice. Add just enough water to cover bottom of pan.
4. Bake at 375°F (190°C) until well-done (about 45 minutes, 175°F [80°C] internal temperature), turning once or twice during baking. (To add colour and crispness, remove a few minutes early and barbeque to desired colour.)
5. *Optional*: To create a dipping sauce, degrease pan juices and simmer until thickened.

22

Must-Have

It must be hellish to feel compelled to have the very latest thing. From the fashion runways of Paris to the convention stages where the latest iGadget is unveiled, marketers pray to the god Mammon that the mere appearance of the New Thing will trigger the must-have-that response in consumers. Even people shackled to three-year cellphone contracts have admitted they'd be willing to pay the financial penalty for breaking them because it frees them...to buy the New Thing. Who wants to hold an ancient (i.e., older than six months) mobile device in public, where people cannot only see, but almost smell, the reek of obsolescence? The shame, the shame.

The captains of the automobile industry mastered "planned obsolescence" in design half a century ago, radically changing the look of car models every year. Each September, the new model (smaller or larger fins, different grille, new colour palette) notified the world that your jalopy was literally *so* last year. But even in Detroit's heyday, if the sales team lured you into the showroom, you could at least "kick the tires"—a phrase that became a metaphor for physically examining what someone was trying to sell you. These days, if you're a slave to the new, you can't even wait for something you can touch or taste or smell. Based on ads, you "pre-order" the thing, because the virtue of newness trumps such quaint notions as necessity or evidence of quality. Such foolish consumer behaviour is historically known as buying a "pig in a poke," a phrase used as early as the sixteenth century to denote someone stupid enough to buy a squirming animal in a sack without inspecting the critter.

But can you be enslaved to the old? Today, I'm staying close to my phone (land line, of course), waiting to hear if I have the winning bids in a silent auction on a dual cassette deck and a turntable.

The running joke in the family is that the only thing I'm leaving the kids is my cassette collection, which currently provides an insulation value of about R12 on the basement wall. But those little tapes need a playback device, and as you might have noticed, cassette decks haven't been front-page news in electronic stores' flyers since the last millennium. So when I heard about this silent auction, I jumped. Simply put, it would have been selfish of me to shuffle off this mortal coil and leave three siblings squabbling over not only the priceless bootlegged David Lindley & El-Rayo-X tapes, but my two cassette decks as well. Three children, two decks? Move over, King Lear.

But what about the turntable? That's a different story, isn't it? While I have two non-functional turntables bought at yard sales ("As Is, Where Is" can usually be translated as "Probably Broken, Sucker"), vinyl, old and new, wants to be heard. Digital music flows in a torrent of downloads, but these days, no self-respecting indie musician would dare drop a new release without a vinyl option, too. And yes, turntable manufacturing has survived its near-death experience.

This wasn't supposed to happen. The new was supposed to annihilate the old. CDs were supposed to make cassettes and LPs the latest in a long line of audio losers stretching back to the Edison wax cylinder. Digital downloads may have undermined CD sales, but there's still a healthy trade in those shiny discs. With music, it seems to have turned into a game of rock, paper, scissors: anything can win.

And while I'm at it, why do people still listen to radio (that thing without the TV pictures)? There's a reason that every new car in the world is equipped with one.

When it comes to my "heritage-format" music, though, I know the prudent thing would be to migrate all those analog tapes and LPs to digital, so I can leave my kids three identical thumb drives of the undivided audio detritus of their dad's life, thus preventing fist fights over who gets the Mory Kanté, who gets the Mahavishnu Orchestra, and who gets the mixtapes. But in the meantime, I'm hoping my silent auction bids land a new-to-me turntable and at least one cassette deck that will see me out.

It's hellish to feel compelled to have the latest Old Thing.

Some foods can be like a favourite tune or artist: you forget about them for years and then feel joy when you rediscover them. I was originally introduced to lentils in Fakorizo (*fa-KO-ree-zo*), the Greek version of a dish that's made in many variations around the Eastern Mediterranean: Sauté an onion and a garlic clove in olive oil in a pot, toss in 1 cup brown lentils and ⅓ cup white rice, stir them to blend the flavours, add two cups of water, bring to a boil, back off to a simmer, stir occasionally until the rice and lentils are cooked, add salt and pepper, and Haralambos (a Greek name often shortened to Bobby) is your uncle. Hot or cold, I loved Fakorizo as a kid—couldn't get enough.

I drifted away from lentils when I went to college, but every four or five years since, I find a recipe that lets me rediscover how much I enjoy their taste and texture. Becoming acquainted with Panch Phoran got me back on a lentil jag. The most popular masala in Bengal, its name simply means "five spices": cumin, fenugreek, mustard seed, fennel, and nigella. No grinding required. Roast dry in a hot pan, or, as in this recipe, fry in hot oil until spices turn reddish-brown and crunchy.

Country-style Lentil Soup with Panch Phoran

Panch Phoran, Chili Peppers, Smoked Sweet Spanish Paprika

SERVES 4

4 tablespoons olive oil
1 tablespoon Panch Phoran
1 onion, chopped
1 celery stalk, diced
1 poblano chili, diced *or* 1 ancho rojo chili, rehydrated and sliced, *or* 1 green pepper, diced
2 tablespoons Smoked Sweet Spanish Paprika
2 tomatoes, chopped
1 bay leaf
2 cups cooked lentils
salt to taste

Garnishes

2 cloves garlic, grated
1 handful fresh cilantro, chopped
½ of 1 chopped onion
3 tablespoons red wine vinegar

1. Heat olive oil over medium heat in large pot. Add Panch Phoran and fry until seeds are light brown (20–30 seconds).
2. Add onion, celery, and chili. Sauté well (8–10 minutes).
3. Add smoked paprika and sauté 2 minutes longer before adding tomatoes, bay leaf, lentils, salt, and enough water to make a hearty soup.
4. Simmer for 30 minutes.
5. While soup simmers, mix grated garlic, chopped cilantro and onion, and red wine vinegar in a bowl. Stir well.
6. Serve soup. Place bowl of chopped onion, cilantro, grated garlic, and red wine vinegar on the table so each person can garnish to taste.

Swiss Chard with Panch Phoran

Panch Phoran, Ginger

SERVES 4

When it comes to my relationship with Swiss chard…it's complicated. I love to see it arrive at the Historic Farmers' Market: gorgeous sprays of big, green bumpy leaves with scarlet or white stems, although some varieties have deep purple leaves and stems in orange, gold, or pink. But as eye-catching as it is, I always find excuses not to buy it. Cooking plans call for other vegetables. They'd never fit in the fridge. They'd wilt on the countertop and look absurd in a flower vase while they wait to be used…someday.

The truth is, I've never given much thought to anything beyond steaming Swiss chard like some overgrown spinach. That's fine, given the nutritional benefits, but it means I've had a culinary blind spot.

This recipe changed that. You can make it as a side dish or meze, but if you want a delicious vegetable soup, just double the amount of tomatoes. When Swiss chard isn't in season, use spinach.

panch phoran

1 pound Swiss chard *or* spinach, chopped
2 tablespoons olive oil
2 teaspoons Panch Phoran
1 onion, chopped
2 teaspoons chopped fresh ginger
1 cup peeled or canned tomatoes (more if you want it soupy)
salt to taste
1 teaspoon ground black pepper
½ cup plain yoghurt
2 tablespoons crème fraîche or heavy (35%) cream
1 garlic clove, grated
1 teaspoon sugar

1. Clean and wash Swiss chard. Drain well in salad spinner.
2. Heat oil on medium heat in large pot and caramelize Panch Phoran (10–15 seconds).
3. Add chopped onion and ginger. Sauté for 5 minutes.
4. Add tomatoes, salt, and black pepper. Cook for 5 minutes.
5. Add Swiss chard. Cook 5 minutes more, stirring regularly.
6. Put yoghurt, crème fraîche, garlic, sugar, and additional salt in a bowl. Whisk vigorously for 1 minute, or until very smooth.
7. Add yoghurt mixture to pot and stir until heated through (1–2 minutes). Serve hot.

Again, this can be served as a soup, or, if you go with less tomato, as a vegetarian side dish. It's also delicious with white fish, such as haddock or sole.

23

How Lucky Can You Get?

It's high summer, with the kind of succession of sun-filled days that exists more in the imaginations of Maritimers than in memories.

This time in 2011, the grapes that grow over my back deck were already showing signs of black rot, which thrives in cool temperatures and wet conditions. But in 2012 I couldn't complain. Thanks to the nearly Mediterranean weather, the grapes were the picture of health. Downtown, restaurant patios were filled day and night, the chatter of patrons blending with the whirr of a thousand credit card machines rolling out receipts. The forecast for the Tall Ships Festival in the Halifax/Dartmouth Harbour was perfect. Darn, we couldn't even complain about the weather.

So what to complain about? As it turned out, local media were filling time and column inches in a slow news period with whiny, victimless complaints (the Tall Ships "aren't tall enough," "Breaking News" that annual road construction slows traffic, etc.).

But let's cut to the chase: life is pretty good for most of us, most of the time. By "us," I mean you and me—people who can afford to buy a book and pay for an Internet connection.

There are setbacks, of course. The social side of my spice trade means that over time, my customers and I get to know each other better. If it's not busy, we may even choose to confide what's happened in our lives since the last visit. There may have been illness, job loss, the breakup of a long relationship, the death of a parent or partner. But by and large, it's a light conversational catch-up between people coasting on the fact that they've won the global lottery by living in Canada.

In my quiet neighbourhood, garbage day is a weekly reminder that not every Canadian is reaping the benefits of living here. Thursday morning birdsong is accompanied by the sound of a wobbly-wheeled shopping cart rolling by with bags of recyclable containers. The operator had just passed this week when I stepped out of the house. He stopped and asked (with a politeness exceeding anything I've noticed among paid retail staff lately) whether I had any bottles. I was already running late driving my wife to work and the bottles and cans I had were in the basement, so I weaseled out a lame, *Sorry. Not this week.* (Mental note: put out a bag of those bottles and cans next time.)

People who collect discarded recyclables certainly meet the criteria of being hard-working and entrepreneurial, but I don't see them getting any kudos in the business media, do you? Or did I miss them being lauded in the Lifestyle pages for their gruelling urban fitness regime? Not a chance. Do they get interviewed by reporters for their thoughts on the economy? Nope. They are more conveniently rendered…invisible.

What does that say about empathy? In most countries, the "haves" are zooming away from the growing numbers of "have-nots" at the speed of light. A 2012 article by Lisa Miller in *New York Magazine* explored "The Money-Empathy Gap," which touches on the "invisibility" reflex. She highlighted the findings of psychologist Paul Piff, whose research included observing the behaviour of pairs of participants playing rigged Monopoly games. In a trial that Miller observed, one player got two thousand dollars of Monopoly money to start, rolled two dice for each turn, and picked up two hundred dollars every time he passed *Go*. The other started with one thousand dollars, was only allowed to roll one die, and collected one hundred dollars for his less-frequent trips past *Go*. In less than fifteen minutes, the player with the unfair advantage moved from slight embarrassment (at the obvious inequity of "the game"), through jocular arrogance (noisily snapping his marker—a Rolls-Royce—with each move), to the final stage—a chilling indifference. He stopped making eye contact with the other player, his expression "stone cold as he [took] the loser's cash."

Don't get me wrong—these dark reflections on a fine summer day don't mean I have a personal dark cloud following me around like Joe Btfsplk, the character in the old *Li'l Abner* cartoon strip. I'm revelling in this season's pleasures as much as anyone. But I'm not so enamoured with the media's breezy "fun in the sun" narrative that I need to airbrush out people or issues that don't fit into it. Instead, I see more and more reasons to be thankful for what I get to enjoy—so much of it the result of pure, dumb luck.

The *Li'l Abner* comic strip mentioned above was created by Al Capp and ran in newspapers for a phenomenal forty-three years, until 1977. Capp satirized society through a huge cast of hillbilly characters in a backwoods community called Dogpatch. He also invented numerous fantastical creatures that embodied human needs and desires (the Bald Iggle could make politicians, lawyers, and car salesmen blurt out the truth by looking them in the eye).

The basic need for food was satisfied by the Shmoo. You didn't have to feed it, but it gave everything from milk (in the bottle, if you please) to eggs. Depending on how you cooked it, it could taste like steak, pork, or chicken. Well, sadly, we don't have shmoos. But chicken seems to be the closest thing to the mythical critter, mainly because it can adapt to any style of cooking and has the knack of absorbing the flavours of whichever herbs or spices you use to prepare it.

Peppercorn Chicken

Serves 4

Peppercorns, Coriander, Cumin, Green Indian Cardamom

This chicken recipe allows pepper to move from its usual supporting role to the spotlight. Use your favourite peppercorns or peppercorn blends (e.g., Lemon Pepper or Eight Pepper). By the way, if you're using "pink peppercorns," don't put them through the peppermill. While tasty and a visual delight, they're not true peppercorns and their resins can gum up the works. You can grind them in a mortar and pestle, or better yet, sprinkle them on whole when you serve the chicken.

2 pounds chicken pieces
3 tablespoons ground peppercorns
2 tablespoons ground coriander
1 teaspoon ground cumin
2 tablespoons ground Green Indian Cardamom seeds, husks discarded
4 tablespoons ghee *or* a mixture of butter and vegetable oil
3 medium tomatoes, peeled and diced
1 small bouquet fresh chopped coriander
salt to taste

1 Remove skin and excess fat from chicken pieces.
2 Wash chicken under running water. Drain and blot dry with paper towel. Place in a bowl.
3 Add ground spices and cover chicken evenly.
4 Heat a large frying pan over medium heat; add ghee.
5 Brown chicken on all sides, turning regularly (10–15 minutes).
6 Add tomatoes, fresh coriander, and salt.
7 Cover and let simmer until chicken is cooked and cooking juices have been well reduced.
8 Serve with root vegetables. Toss them in vegetable oil and either dried herbs or a mix, like Za'atar, and roast them at 375°F (190°C) for about an hour and a quarter. The caramelized vegetables and herbs make a nice contrast with the spicy, juicy chicken.

24

Fighting Words

What would it take to provoke you to anger? A driver cutting you off? Someone insulting your mother? A slap in the face? For many Maritimers, all it takes is someone from another part of Canada to slag this region in public.

Such was the case when the *Globe and Mail* published the transcript of Alexandra Gill's phone interview with Jacob Richler, who was promoting his book *My Canada Includes Foie Gras*. It began with the obligatory reference by Richler *fils* to his father Mordecai: novelist, freelance writer extraordinaire, and full-time provocateur. Eventually, we get to this:

> *The book is primarily focused on Quebéc, Ontario and British Columbia. The Prairies and the Atlantic provinces get short shrift. Don't they offer anything to Canadian cuisine?*
>
> *They have lots to offer. They just haven't discovered it yet. The Maritimes is a culinary sad sack, or at least it has been for years. Their crimes against seafood are particularly egregious. It's changing. This summer, I had a seafood platter at Raymonds in St. John's that was lightly done and the lobster was tender. But in terms of the deadline for this book, it was too late.*

It doesn't take a close reading of the patronizing reply to make you wince—or perhaps to piss you off. Even if you don't live here, you can spot the fact that Richler is guilty of "burying the lede"—that is, the last sentence in the reply is the most significant.

It was too late is also ambiguous. Does this mean Richler couldn't afford to wait the years it might take for benighted Maritimers to create restaurants that met his standards? Did it mean he hadn't done anything resembling basic research here? Or were those nasty editors and their damned deadlines to blame for an arbitrary, slapdash review of what's good and what isn't in Canadian dining?

The release of Richler's book dovetailed with the publication of *Maclean's* magazine's "The 50 Best Restaurants in Canada," which he compiled, "based on a calendar year that, due to our fall publishing date, starts and ends at Canada Day." Darn. Another deadline. Seven Maritime restaurants made the list—arguably, not bad. But do you agree with the choices?

Whether they're about restaurants or rock guitarists, "Best" lists spit like hot fat, burning anyone whose favourite isn't included. As the *Maclean's* introduction puts it, *however much work and good sense goes into such things, they are seldom praised and always attacked—and gleefully.* In other words, "Best" lists create argumentative buzz, and buzz is good for sales. The introduction then waffles along to say, *we will come right out and admit that when rated exclusively on traditional merits, scored only on what they put on the plate, and how they serve it, the restaurants included here may not be our absolute 50 best.*

Ah. This is only "The 50 Best Restaurants in Canada," not "The Absolute 50 Best Restaurants in Canada." That would have cost more, I guess, or at least a re-definition of "Best." So with all the caveats, a better title would have been, "50 Pretty Good Restaurants (Sorry About the Excellent Ones We Didn't Get Around to Trying)."

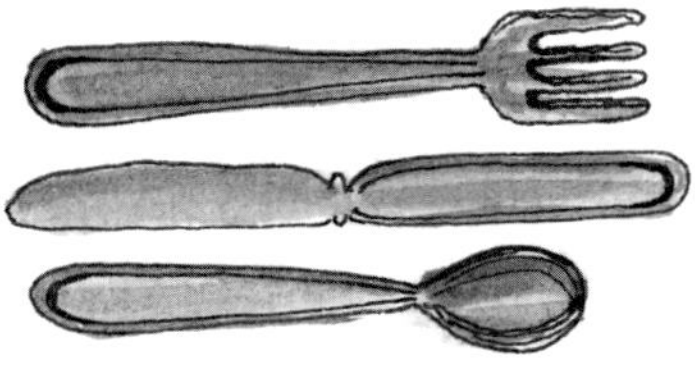

Getting back to Richler's description of our region as "a culinary sad sack," it lacks the hostile edge of "Let the Eastern bastards freeze in the dark" (Ralph Klein, then mayor of Calgary, later premier of Alberta), or Stephen Harper's alluding to what he saw as our region's "culture of defeat." It does, however, fit the familiar pattern of casually stereotyping the Maritimes from a distance. The only dish Richler mentions in the interview is, of course, seafood—probably caught by those quaint fishermen in their quaint boats, which they tie up to quaint wharves in quaint villages.

It's easy to rise to the bait of taunts like these (or Klein's or Harper's). It's annoying to be dismissed as people too stupid to "discover" what we have here (it takes a culinary Columbus to do that). It's irksome to be libelled as people who commit "egregious" crimes against seafood (*No, Angus—you don't waterboard the haddock! You burn them with cigarettes!).* But there's no need to add "thin-skinned" to our long list of deficiencies. That just plays into the game of creating buzz.

The fact is the Maritimes will always be doomed to getting short shrift in unscientific "national" surveys. When food writers based in Montréal, Toronto, or Vancouver aren't on assignment, they're just a few Metro stops or a cab ride away from more restaurants than we have in all three provinces. They can check out a new bistro or three in their hometown every week, and given the failure rate in the industry, be assured of a steady stream of replacements to feed their appetite for novelty.

What's lost in the assumption that "nothing happens in the hinterlands" is the fact that everybody in a creative industry like the restaurant business knows what's going on everywhere in the world. Chat with a Maritime restaurateur or chef for a minute and you'll realize how often they travel to research new techniques, ingredients, and trends. And yes, they have access to the Interwebs. When it comes to food writers taking brief expeditions away from well-travelled turf, though, publishers' travel budgets aren't generous enough to pay for the kind of extended stays that encourage the "discovery" of great cuisine at (fill in your favourite restaurants here).

So when it comes to glib smears of all the talented chefs in the Maritimes, don't get angry. Instead, go out and savour the best you can afford in one of their restaurants. And don't pass up an opportunity to tell people outside the region what they're missing.

Renée's Chorizo and Okra Gumbo

Okra, Allspice, Dried Chili Peppers

SERVES 6

Speaking of talented chefs in the region, this flavourful one-pot dinner is the creation of the indefatigable Renée Lavallée. After leaving a full-time executive chef position to have a more flexible schedule with her family, she's become an in-demand guest chef at many seasonal and community dinners and culinary showcases. Her blog, Feisty Chef, exudes her puckish humour and engaging approach to cooking, while championing the best local food suppliers.

Renée's gumbo is perfect for a casual meal with family or friends. Okra isn't as rare as it once was in most Maritime produce sections, and there's a wealth of local artisanal-sausage makers, such as Sweet William's Country Sausage (in several farmers' markets) or Jessi Gillis's Highland Drive Storehouse (in Halifax's Hydrostone district), who tackle myriad international styles from French andouille and Greek loukaniko to the Spanish-style chorizo you'll need for this recipe.

Allspice is the only spice you need. Its complexity can keep your taste buds guessing which of its many flavour notes you're tasting with each new bite. The heat is supplied by the dried chili of your choice, from the tiny piquin to habanero or the smoky but milder chipotle grande.

4 tablespoons vegetable oil
1 onion, diced
2 garlic cloves, minced
4 chorizo sausages, crumbled
4 ribs of celery, diced
dried chili peppers to taste
1 red pepper, diced
6 small new potatoes, diced
2–3 teaspoons ground allspice
8–12 okra, thickly sliced
1 pint of grape tomatoes
4 cups chicken stock
½ cup white rice
1 cup chopped fresh cilantro, divided
Juice of 2 limes

1. Heat a large, heavy-bottomed pot and add a small amount of vegetable oil. Sauté diced onion, then, briefly, the garlic.
2. Add crumbled chorizo. Brown.
3. Add celery, chili peppers, red pepper, diced potatoes, and—if necessary—additional oil. Add allspice; cook 4–5 minutes.
4. Add okra and tomatoes. Sauté 2–3 minutes.
5. Add stock. Check seasoning and adjust if needed.
6. Bring to a boil and add rice. Lower to a simmer.
7. Add ½ the cilantro. Simmer until rice and potato are cooked through.
8. Add lime juice and remaining cilantro.

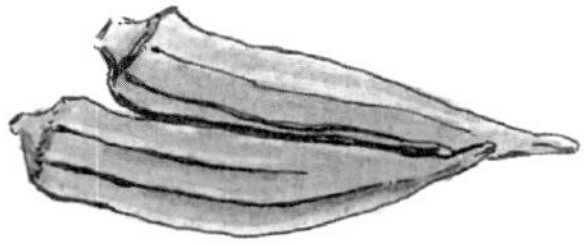

okra

25

The Big Exit

Comedians work hard for their laughs, but there's nothing like unintentional humour to make you spit out your morning coffee.

The other day when I was reading the newspaper, I spotted an ad for a national chain of funeral homes. For clients who wanted a "pre-arranged funeral" (which I presume is the alternative to the Panicked, Hastily Arranged Funeral), the chain was now offering…Air Miles.

For reasons known only to my subconscious, the logo of that cheery little airplane in a funeral home ad got me smiling. But before I had a chance to figure out why, the ad hit me with a follow-up, just the way a skilled comedian gets you chuckling before delivering the punch line that triggers uncontrollable guffaws.

There in the corner of the ad was the logo of the funeral home chain: *Dignity.*

I lost it.

Was it the image of the comically chubby, blue airplane juxtaposed with the black, sober-fonted *Dignity*? Was it a question about whether you could use Air Miles for a one-way trip to destinations in the afterlife? Who knows?

I do know there's nothing more inexplicable than what strikes someone as funny. I also know that anything pertaining to death is especially rich comic territory (notice that I tastefully did not use the phrase "fertile ground"). Think about how many sitcoms and movie scenes revolved around the characters meeting at a funeral or memorial service. We've even had *Death: The Musical.* Death delivers natural tension, stretched to the breaking point. On one side: profound emotions and rigid societal expectations of decorum. On the other:

the absurd, looking for an opportunity to break through with a clown nose and a kazoo.

Real funerals and memorial services aren't immune to this. I've been to plenty, and if demographics mean anything, I'll be attending even more before I find myself in the one that won't matter to me at all. Despite the headline act (The Deceased), these events are more about the living than the dead. If the relationship to the person who has died was bad, people sit in their pews trying to sort through a perverse combination of emotional knots and loose ends.

I've attended services ranging from the utterly impersonal to such maudlin outpourings that I just wanted to crawl into a casket (preferably unoccupied) and close the lid. At some, the surviving family members looked so physically devastated, it was as if their very bones had been dissolved by the loss. I've left some services angry. At others, though, the smiles and patter were more what you'd expect at a wedding. Certain stories had everyone laughing out loud in recognition of some truth about the departed—generally, a person who was secure enough when living to enjoy being the butt of affectionate teasing and jokes. Services like these leave me feeling strangely uplifted.

Recently, I attended a service for the mother of a friend and former colleague. Children and grandchildren spoke, briefly (always a virtue) and eloquently (a bonus). They had all been immersed in this woman's love their entire lives, and it had obviously shaped their characters and approaches to life. Representatives from different faith traditions spoke without turning their comments into religious commercials. There was well-chosen, well-performed music. And it wasn't an airbrushed event: there were matter-of-fact references to the sorrows and setbacks that come with every life. But overall, there emerged a consistent picture of a woman who—despite having a huge circle of family, friends, and acquaintances over more than eight decades—presented the same generous spirit to all. They would leave this service carrying what she had imparted to them when she was alive. And while there were elements of grief and loss in the air that day, the goodness of her life clearly triumphed.

Way to go, indeed. And a reminder of how we, the living, should live.

Jambalaya

Cajun Spices

SERVES 4

AiyEEE! is a life-affirming yell. I heard it hollered many, many times (or, more properly, *minny, minny tams*) at a gig in Halifax's venerable Resolutes Club, which featured the legendary Louisiana fiddler and singer Waylon Thibodeaux. He was accompanied by his father, Elgin, on *frottoir* (a metal rub-board worn like a vest and played with spoons to great percussive effect) and his friend Jimmy Thibodeaux on Cajun accordion. Dancers from ages twenty to eighty hit the floor. The band played a great version of that lyrically brilliant, musically infectious Hank Williams song, "Jambalaya," so why resist this cosmic cue?

I've attached my friend Guy's recipe for the classic, one-pot Louisiana meal that gives the song its name. Jambalaya is ideal at any time of the year. It features the salt-free Cajun Spices (if you add salt, you can use it in Cajun recipes that call for "blackening" meat or fish).

One secret of great Jambalaya is the way hot chicken fat coats the rice so it keeps its texture during long cooking. Locally produced chorizo sausage adds a subtle smoked aroma to the rich flavour of local free-range chicken. Also, unpeeled shrimp imparts a stronger taste than peeled.

4 skin-on free-range whole chicken legs
2 tablespoons vegetable oil
2 medium-sized yellow onions, diced
1 red or green bell pepper, diced
2 smoked sausages (I like Sweet William's at the Historic Farmers' Market)
1 cup diced ham
4 cloves garlic, minced
4 scallions with tops, sliced
1½ cups long-grain rice, rinsed
2 tablespoons (*or more*) Cajun Spices Blend
3 cups boiling hot chicken stock *or* water
salt to taste
½ pound raw shrimp

1. Cut chicken legs into thigh and drumstick. Pat dry. Sauté until golden; set aside.
2. In same pan, sauté yellow onion and green pepper until soft.
3. Slice sausages in ¾-inch pieces. Add sausage and diced ham to pan and continue cooking until they start to brown.
4. Add minced garlic, sliced scallions, rice, and Cajun Spices. Cook, stirring, until rice starts to turn opaque, 2–3 minutes.
5. Add hot stock (or water) and salt. Return chicken to pan, cover, and bring to a low simmer. Cook at very low heat for 30 minutes.
6. Adjust seasoning
7. Stir in raw shrimp. Continue cooking until chicken and shrimp are fully cooked, 15–20 minutes longer, adding some liquid, if needed, to keep rice moist.
8. Serve with lemon wedges and plenty of freshly ground rich black pepper, such as Tellicherry Saji's Estate Extra Bold or Extra Extra Bold (designations that relate to size, rather than heat).

26

Cookbooks and Olympics

I really try not to succumb to the lure of additional cookbooks. But I fail, over and over again. Just as you did when you bought the one you're holding (*gotcha!*).

There are so many ways they seduce you. Oh, it's easy to ignore the come-hither look of an expensive hardcover with eye-popping colour photographs of artfully composed dishes. But when it's discounted by 75 per cent, it becomes irresistible. "Cheap and easy," defined.

Did I need another cookbook on Greek cuisine? Of course not…until my friend Bob showed me the fascinating *New Greek Cuisine* by Aristedes Pasparakis and bon vivant Byron Ayanoglu—and then gave it to me. My rationalization for accepting Bob's generosity? I can now invite friends to pop in for a plate of *Ageopelagiotiki Astakomakaronatha* (which is fun and surprisingly easy to say; try it—Greek is entirely phonetic). Basically, it's pasta with a simple tomato/lobster sauce: traditional ingredients in Greece's Aegean Islands, with a modern accent.

"Basically." That was a word I desperately tried to avoid when I used to work in radio, because it can become an annoying verbal tic. But it's been on my mind a lot lately. There are decidedly non-basic recipes sporting a list of ingredients the length of your arm—ingredients gradually introduced over hours or even days of preparation through more stages than a decathlon, and which, admittedly, yield a delicious dish.

But c'mon, the Law of Diminishing Returns kicks in at some point. Who has that amount of time to spend in a kitchen if you're not being paid to work there? And there's a limit to deliciousness, just as there's a limit to how high an athlete can jump before gravity beckons. I'm suspicious that the real point of taking on one of these fancy marathon culinary events is to impress guests.

As with cookbooks, it's interesting to contrast what you might call "basic" and "fancy" Olympic events. Basic footraces, as ancient as the Olympics themselves, always fill the host stadium. And even though we now employ high-speed cameras for "photo finishes," the point of the contest is the same: the fastest person wins. No fancy schmancy subjective, political (and occasionally corrupt) judging.

At the same time, the aristocratic and inscrutable International Olympic Committee has allowed utterly artificial sports into the Games. Consider the absurd Canoe/Kayak Slalom. I think it was dreamed up by dope-smokers at an especially mellow *après-ski* one winter evening in Gstaad, when Hans passed the spliff to Fritz and said, *Dude—imagine if all the snow on the Matterhorn melted man, and instead of skis, you had to do the slalom in a freaking canoe!* To which Fritz responded, *Heavy….* And Hans replied, *Whaa?*

Regardless of how it started, it became a fixture in Barcelona in 1992. According to the IOC website, it is "conducted on flowing water, rushing down a steep course where competitors attempt to negotiate a slalom course in single runs against the clock."

Right. I know a glorified 1980s roadside-attraction waterslide when I see one, complete with plastic sluices, fibreglass rocks, electro-hydraulic pumps and water jets. As for the IOC argument that it wants to include more "exciting and modern sports that attract younger people" (i.e., people who watch TV narrated by commentators hooked up to an IV drip of Red Bull), Canoe/Kayak Slalom is as interesting on TV as watching a toy boat slosh around in a washing machine. There's no discernible forward progress. It's boring.

More insidiously, only a rich country can afford to build a course on which its Canoe/Kayak Slalom athletes can train for this "sport." Take my word on this: Haiti and Somalia will not be competing in this event in the foreseeable future. And as for a rising Olympic tide raising all boats, the IOC's "Sport

For All" initiative (as far as I can tell from its own media releases) is superbly successful at holding conferences, where experts fly in, talk, are wined and dined by the country that wants to ingratiate itself with the IOC, and fly back home.

Perhaps Jamaica is dominating in traditional—and infinitely more compelling—Olympic sports like the sprints because it's poor, and the original sports are so accessible to everyone. This ensures there's a huge national base of competitors to draw upon, yielding one Usain Bolt.

So whether we like such potentially enjoyable pastimes as watching the Olympics or cooking, we still have to negotiate conflicting layers of complexity and spin, not to mention issues of class and economics. Whether our understanding and motivations are basic or fancy, our work is cut out for us.

Ageopelagiotiki Astakomakaronatha (Aegean Islands-style Lobster Pasta)

Dionysios' Wild Herb Blend, Italian Parsley

SERVES 4

You didn't think I was going to mention that without sharing the recipe, did you? Especially since it comes from the birthplace of the Olympics.... If you're squeamish about lobster tamale/tomalley (the mushy green liver, under the carapace/shell), skip this recipe. Pasparakis is fond of using non-stick pans with no fat (not even EVOO from Greece!). He prefers to use the olive oil on its own—uncompromised by heat—in dressings with lemon juice, or in sauces.

2 cups thinly sliced leek (white part only) *or* chopped green onion
4 cloves garlic, minced
3 cups fresh plum tomatoes, diced
2–4 (1¼ pound) live lobsters
1 pound linguine
1 cup dry white wine (retsina—the much-maligned, light wine from the Athens region, with its hint of pine from the barrel—would be a nice touch)
salt and freshly ground pepper to taste
1 cup chopped fresh Italian parsley
1 tablespoon Dionysios' Wild Herb Blend
½ cup ouzo
¼ cup extra-virgin olive oil (I'm very fond of peppery Greek Koroneiki, available at Liquid Gold shops around the Maritimes and Vicki Buckley's Shop On The Corner in Lunenburg)

1. Bring a large pot of salted water to a boil.
2. This will take a while, so in the meantime, dice tomatoes and put in a bowl; chop leek and garlic and place in a separate bowl.
3. Plunge lobsters into boiling water and cook, 8–10 minutes.
4. Drain and cool lobsters for 15 minutes. Save hot water for linguine.
5. Take apart lobsters: Tear off legs and claws. Break claws with a lobster-cracker (sorry, but dainty nutcrackers aren't up to the job—the physics are all wrong). Reserve claws and legs.
6. Shell tail, devein, and rinse. Slice tail meat into ½-inch-thick medallions. Reserve.
7. Lift off the carapace (back shell). Scoop out the "tomalley" (digestive gland) with a spoon and put it in a small bowl. With a lobster- or walnut-pick, extract the little pieces of white meat from the back and add to the tomalley. Blend until smooth and reserve.

8 Cook linguine in boiling salted water until al dente, 8–10 minutes; drain.

9 Heat a large non-stick frying pan on high for about 3 minutes. Toss in leek and garlic and cook, stirring, for a couple of minutes. Add tomatoes, wine, Dionysios' Wild Herb Blend, pepper, and salt to taste. Cook on high heat 4–5 minutes until mixture begins to thicken as a sauce. Reduce heat to medium.

10 Add blended tomalley mixture, tail medallions, parsley, ouzo, and olive oil. Cook 2–3 minutes, stirring gently, while alcohol evaporates. Do not let sauce boil.

11 Add linguine to sauce and fold, coating the pasta.

12 Serve immediately, garnished with reserved claws and legs, crusty bread, and a crisp, dry white wine.

Pastitsio

Cinnamon, White Pepper, Nutmeg

SERVES 8

This traditional Greek casserole has become a cherished homecoming meal for our prodigal children. Often, I mix half ground beef and half ground lamb.

Equipment

frying pan
large pot for pasta
double boiler for Mornay sauce
2½-quart baking dish, oiled

Meat Sauce

1 large onion, chopped
4 cloves garlic, minced
1½ pounds lean ground beef
2 tablespoons olive oil
A few pinches salt
1 teaspoon ground cinnamon
1 (8 ounce) can tomato sauce

Mornay Sauce

3 tablespoons melted butter
¼ cup flour
2 cups milk
½ teaspoon salt
A few pinches white pepper
1 teaspoon ground nutmeg
⅓ cup Parmesan

Macaroni

2 eggs

2 cups macaroni

2 tablespoons butter

2 cups shredded hard white cheese (Kefalotiri if possible, but Romano will do)

Method

Meat Sauce

1. Sauté onion at medium heat until translucent. Add garlic.
2. Add ground beef, stirring until nearly cooked, but still slightly pink.
3. Stir in a pinch salt, a few dashes cinnamon, and tomato sauce. Turn off heat and set aside (meat will finish cooking while Pastitsio is baking).

Mornay Sauce

1. Melt 3 tablespoons butter in top of double boiler. Keep water in bottom half just simmering: do not boil.
2. Whisk in the flour and mix with melted butter.
3. Add milk, bit by bit, whisking regularly as the sauce thickens.
4. Add salt, white pepper, a few dashes nutmeg, and the Parmesan.
5. Turn heat to low and allow sauce to mellow, whisking occasionally.

Macaroni

1. Scramble eggs in a bowl.
2. Cook macaroni about 10 minutes and drain.
3. Put 2 tablespoons butter in the empty, but still-warm pot. Return macaroni and combine with butter.
4. Add scrambled eggs and mix well with a wooden spoon.

Assembly

Layer ingredients in the following order in oiled baking dish:

1 ½ Macaroni
2 Meat Sauce
3 ½ hard cheese
4 rest of Macaroni
5 Mornay Sauce (whisk again before pouring)
6 Shake the dish gently to settle the sauce. Add the rest of the hard cheese. Drop on a few dabs of butter and a few sprinkles of nutmeg.
7 If tonight's the night, bake at 375°F (190°C)for about 45 minutes to 1 hour. If you're not going to serve the Pastitsio immediately, let it cool down, then cover and refrigerate. Remove from the fridge about ½ hour before baking. Bake for about 75 minutes, or until the top starts to brown.

Serve with Greek red wine. The selections come and go in provincial liquor stores, but look for indigenous Greek grapes, such as Agiorgitiko or Xinomavro, either as varietals or as part of a blend. Add salad, fresh fruit, and cheese, large quantities of good conversation, and lots of impertinent jabs.

27

Recipe Genealogy or Plagiarism?

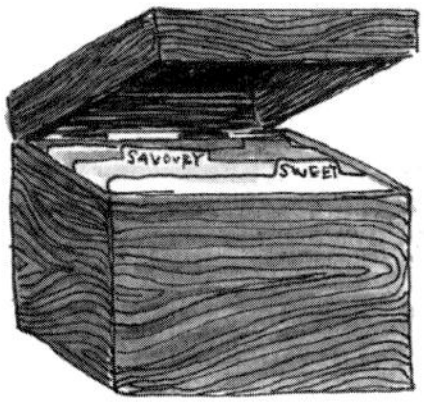

You took the words right out of my mouth!

That's what family or friends say when they acknowledge you beat them to the punch in articulating some thought they just had. It's a compliment—either admiring (*You're quicker than I am*) or self-serving (*Great minds think alike*).

You took the words right out of my text is what people say when they accuse you of plagiarism.

The Canadian news, online, and social media were abuzz in 2012 over a "gotcha" provided by blogger Carol Wainio of the University of Ottawa, a very close reader of Margaret Wente's columns in the *Globe and Mail.* The *Globe* editorial staff had been ignoring Wainio's steady flow of evidence in her blog, Media Culpa, that Wente really, really liked the cut-and-paste function on her computer, but had an aversion towards quotation marks. The reactions of the *Globe*, every other media outlet, and anyone who takes time to blog or comment on associated websites, created a broad discussion on professional standards for attribution of reused material. Wente stood in the corner for a while, and then returned to writing her column; chastened, I hope.

What about recipes, though? Of all the people who cook, relatively few create original recipes. The starting point for a meal you've never tried is usually a printed recipe. If you get good results and repeat the preparation enough times, you become confident enough to start tinkering and improvising with proportions or ingredients.

Let's say you're invited to contribute a favourite recipe to a cookbook project sponsored by a local school, church, or other community group. What exactly do you submit? And if you don't send in a faithful copy of the original along with full credits, do you at least mention where you got the idea in the first place?

If the recipe has evolved enough over the years in your kitchen, what you submit might be akin to a paraphrase of something you once read, not a quote. What I'm trying to figure out is whether I just want to be myself or I want to act like someone I'm not. Who would recognize that as a paraphrase of Shakespeare's "To be or not to be—that is the question."? In fact, it's possible to come up with that statement without ever having read *Hamlet*. Pass the grey paint.

OK. But what if you actually do want to give full credit for your foolproof recipe for Scalloped Potatoes, which you read in a Ladies' Auxiliary cookbook decades ago? And before that, who was the first person to write down a recipe for scalloped potatoes anyway? Good luck, but overall, there's not much in that example that requires a loss of sleep.

Many of the recipes I share come from Philippe and Ethné de Vienne of Spice Trekkers in Montréal, my source for spices. And many of their recipes come from copying down what they observe and what answers they get to questions they ask in kitchens they visit while on their spice hunting expeditions. They aim for authenticity, but some aspects might be modified for Canadian cooks, who aren't always in a position to dig a pit, line it with fresh banana leaves, prepare coals, and…oh, never mind.

Other recipes are created and critiqued in the Spice Trekkers's kitchen in East End Montréal, where the staff gathers for daily lunch. In all cases—from overseas or the staff kitchen—credit is given in the website's recipe section.

My other sources for the weekly recipes are cookbooks, friends, and…the Internet.

Ah, the Internet. While I always give credit for recipes, I've found that researching the source of one can be like trying to find the original composer of a well-known tune (and thanks to my pal Rob who alerted me to the important fact that "[Big Old] Jet Airliner" was written by Paul Pena, not Steve Miller). As with music, there can be many cover versions of a recipe, and often, it's an interpreter—not the creator—who gets the unofficial credit. How many restaurants that offer "Caesar Salad" credit the creator? But in music publishing, there are strict standards for giving credit, and as the late George Harrison found out, you can be sued successfully for, ahem, "appropriating" a melody. Twelve-bar blues, though? More grey paint.

I ran into the recipe-related parallel when researching a recipe for Grains of Paradise (guinea peppers), a spice adorned in colourful historical lore. I found one for a cocktail called "Bloody Paradise" on a foodie website (see p. 92). Some friends and I tested the recipe. And tested it again. It was a cocktail, after all. But mainly, I was suspicious that the recipe called for too much balsamic vinegar. Thanks to rigorous testing, we established that the prescribed amount was just right. I wrote up the recipe, my friends Guy and Ruth vetted it again, I credited the foodie website, and I sent it out with the newsletter.

Don't ask me why, but I went back to my computer and noodled some more on Grains of Paradise (yes, they're that interesting). That's when I stumbled on a *New York Times* piece, which gave a familiar-looking recipe for "Bloody Paradise." Seems the recipe had actually been concocted by a well-known New York chef and restaurateur called Jean-Georges Vongerichten. My recipe credits have been updated.

Knowing the origin of something that you publish, verbatim, in an article under your own name without attributing the source is a form of theft. Does recipe recycling rank with some of Ms. Wente's capers (or her editor's failures to heed warnings about them)? Perhaps not. Recipes seem to be circulated without much concern for genealogy. I can't recall recipes ever being mentioned in discussions of intellectual property. But why should recipe publishing be exempted from the most basic of ethical considerations: credit where credit's due?

Anyway, I'll sleep with a clear conscience tonight, because I know you'll love the following recipe and the names of the Southern Belles who took credit for it in a now-vintage cookbook.

Broiled Peppercorn Shrimp

Lemon Pepper Blend or Eight Pepper Blend

Serves 4

The Junior Charity League of Monroe, Louisiana, presents their favorite recipes in The Cotton Country Collection. So says the title page of this wonderful 1972 opus from my friend Guy's library of cookbooks, which requires an adjective beyond "eclectic." The book includes Mrs. C. D. Oakley, Jr.'s classic of Deep Southern Cuisine, "Squirrel Mulligan." I know…so many squirrels, so many cultural taboos about eating them. This recipe, however, from Mrs. George Smellings III and Mrs. Jerry Wolff, gives us the chance to showcase flavourful peppercorn blends with shrimp. As you'll see, these women really like their pepper.

1 pound shell-on shrimp (adjust amount based on number of guests)
3 tablespoons olive oil
cracked Lemon Pepper Blend *or* Eight Pepper Blend
salt
juice of 2 lemons
Tabasco sauce to taste
Worcestershire sauce to taste
½ cup butter, cubed

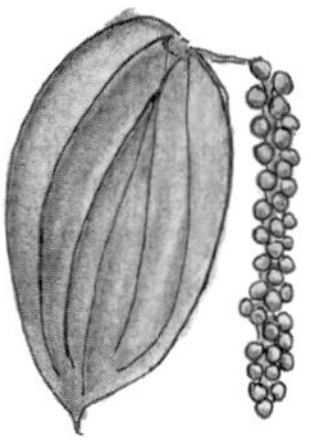

black pepper

1. Place shell-on shrimp in single layer in a shallow, ovenproof dish or baking sheet. Drizzle olive oil over shrimp.
2. Grind pepper blend of choice, or black pepper over shrimp until black. When you think they have enough pepper, add more.
3. Add lots of salt, lemon juice, Tabasco, and Lea and Perrins Worcestershire sauce. Remember: you're seasoning through the shells.
4. Place small cubes of butter on top of shrimp.
5. Broil shrimp until cooked, 5–10 minutes. Test for doneness (shells should be pink and opaque). Peel and devour.

Have lots of napkins and French baguette to sop up the juices. The brave may lick their fingers. Cold beer or wine and green salad complete the meal.

28

Role Players

So, do you get to travel all over the world for these gorgeous spices?

You're standing in front of my table in the familiar Historic Farmers' Market in Halifax, but for a moment our imaginations are transported to the aromatic, technicolour spice markets of Marrakesh, Istanbul (aka Constantinople), Oaxaca, or Alleppey. Towering cones of paprika, bulging panniers of cumin, dangling strings of rare chilies. Shouting vendors. Exotic scents.

But if you're one of the many customers who've asked me that question, you know the answer is *No*. There's no audible sigh, but I will admit to a certain wistfulness at the thought of wandering through faraway souks and bazaars. Don't get me wrong—I'm contented to be in the airy Upper Courtyard of our venerable Halifax market every Saturday morning, coasting vicariously on the work of Philippe and Ethné de Vienne. They actually have been journeying to all those markets and many others for more than twenty-five years. I get to deliver to you what they've brought back to their home base in Montréal.

I'm as intrigued as you are by the spice trade. Its history, however, is not the stuff of breezy travelogues. If you want a disturbing introduction to the trade's influence on exploration, colonization, global politics, the refinement of such recently rediscovered torture techniques as waterboarding, and even genocide, find a copy of Giles Milton's *Nathaniel's Nutmeg: Or the True and Incredible Adventures of the Spice Trader Who Changed the Course of History*. That sprinkle of nutmeg on your cappuccino will never be the same.

But when I retired a few years ago, I wasn't about to cash in my RRSPs and set off to the Banda Islands for nutmeg or the Cardamom Hills in search of, well, cardamom. Others have already done that very well, thank you. No, I'm satisfied to be what's known in team sports as a "role player," or, in movies, a "character actor." I'm driven enough to want to enjoy the rush of being part of a winning team effort and experienced enough to know that stars don't guarantee success. In life, I'm a backup singer, not the front man.

When I worked in radio as a host, I was always (and still am) embarrassed at the public attention automatically given to people in that position. This isn't some "aw, shucks…" assertion of false modesty: my ego is in better shape than my body. But ten minutes behind the scenes on any show—during preparation or execution—and you'd understand how absurd it is to credit that single person with the collective efforts of so many. Ditto for the chef at a top-ranked restaurant, or the principal of a good school. It's not a world of soloists. It's a world of choirs.

It's important to sort that out personally. Challenge yourself? Always. But the inability to assess your capabilities realistically—what you can do on your own and what you can only do with the cooperation and help of others—is a tragic flaw. This is never more apparent than when you watch "candid" backstage interviews with participants in reality show competitions. The sous-chefs who want to elbow their way past peers to become a full-blown Celebrity Chef. Dime-a-dozen singers who believe their overwrought covers of hit tunes will catapult them to stardom—nothing less! "Failure is not an option!" they recite, unconvincingly. The envy. The jealousy. The delusions. It's as if the only dog is the top dog, and if you're not top dog, you might as well be dog food. It makes you want to shout *Get a grip!*

So getting back to my real role in the romance of the international spice trade, I plan no more exotic journeys than the weekly Saturday trek across the harbour bridge, from one part of town to another. No camels, just a 2006 used car. Yes, there is a genuine connection between the markets of India, Mexico, Trinidad, Syria, and Greece and the spices you can sniff and taste at my table. I wish we could travel to the forests of Madagascar where the Voatsiperifery Wild Peppers were picked and to the sheds in Papua New Guinea where the vanilla pods were cured. But for the time being, we'll keep our reveries private and acknowledge our interdependent roles: customer and middleman—that is, until we return to our respective homes and both start cooking with spices.

Smoked Sweet Spanish Paprika

When you find yourself asking, *What's missing?* while you're cooking, you need to call on your "role players." One favourite is Smoked Sweet Spanish Paprika. Here's a list of ideas, but I'm certain you'll find your own uses.

1. Mix with olive oil; rub between the skin and breast of a roast chicken.
2. Prepare sensational beef goulash, spaghetti sauce, and chilies.
3. Add to eggs: devilled eggs, egg salad sandwich, or scrambled eggs.
4. Spice up hot or cold tomato soup.
5. Mix into guacamole dip.
6. Flavour butter with garlic, a pinch of sugar, and smoked paprika.
7. Flavour risotto; top with finely chopped chorizo sausages and tomatoes.
8. Cook in a little olive oil to release flavour. Then mix with extra-virgin olive oil and use to marinate feta cheese.
9. Add a little sweet smoked paprika to a vinaigrette.
10. Sprinkle on thick, plain yoghurt drizzled with olive oil, and serve as a dip.
11. Spice up broccoli, cauliflower, or sautéed zucchini: quickly fry 2 chopped cloves of garlic, 1 teaspoon of sweet smoked paprika and a bay leaf in a little extra-virgin olive oil.

12 Add a splash of wine, apple or pear vinegar to a teaspoon of the paprika, some chopped red onion, and toss it with the steamed vegetables.

13 Slowly fry sliced onions, potatoes, and chopped garlic in olive oil and a little sweet smoked paprika, season well and serve with roast lamb.

14 Rub skinned, boned, firm white fish fillets with a mixture of 2 tablespoons Smoked Sweet Spanish Paprika, ½ teaspoon salt, and the juice of 1 lemon. Dust with flour and fry in hot olive oil until golden.

Sweet Potato, Green Bean, and Smoked Paprika Salad

Smoked Sweet Spanish Paprika, Parsley

SERVES 4

A little bit of Smoked Paprika goes a long way. That's why this recipe only requires two teaspoons despite all those potatoes, tomatoes, and green beans. As with any spice, you don't want it to take centre stage, but rather act in a supporting role for the other ingredients.

3 tablespoons extra-virgin olive oil
1 onion, finely sliced
1 sweet potato, peeled and cut into thick wedges
2 potatoes, cut into thick wedges
2 garlic cloves, finely chopped
2 teaspoons Smoked Sweet Spanish Paprika
1 teaspoon salt
freshly ground black pepper to taste
1 large handful green beans, trimmed and halved
3 ripe tomatoes, cut into wedges
1 handful flat-leaf parsley, chopped
juice of ½ of 1 lemon
Optional: sour cream or natural yoghurt to serve

1 Preheat oven to 400°F (200°C). Heat 3 tablespoons olive oil in ovenproof frying pan over medium heat. Add onion and potatoes and pan-fry 5–10 minutes, tossing occasionally, until lightly browned.

2 Stir in chopped garlic, Smoked Sweet Spanish Paprika, salt, and generous black pepper, coating well. Transfer pan to oven and roast until vegetables are tender, about 15 minutes.

3 Bring a small saucepan of water to boil. Add green beans and simmer for a few minutes, then drain.

4 Put hot green beans into a large bowl with tomato and parsley. Add hot roasted vegetables, lemon juice, and an extra splash of olive oil. Toss to combine. Add extra salt and pepper to taste, if needed.

5 Serve with dollops of sour cream or plain yoghurt if desired.

29

The Anxious Season

It was a raw December afternoon about thirty years ago in Saint John. A damp wind was screaming in off the Bay of Fundy, and if you were on the street, you just wanted to get into a warm, dry place as soon as you could. I was about to open the door to my apartment when I spotted a neighbour—a senior official with the city—trudging up the street. He was holding onto his natty fedora with one hand and a sparking cigarette with the other.

Jack was a delightful guy in his early seventies—a local historian and walking, talking compendium of stories teeming with colourful characters and vignettes of the city's disappearing folkways. I was surprised to see him heading home because I knew the municipality's annual Christmas bash for staff was just getting under way uptown. When I asked why he was passing up all the free snacks and booze with his colleagues, he took a puff, looked up from under the brim of his hat, and said, *I have to work with the* [censored] *all year; I don't have to party with them.*

I'm reminded of that street corner encounter every year when holiday invitations start circulating. Invitations are a mixed bag. Some, like the one Jack was secure enough to blow off, are painful duties. The small talk. The schoolyard cliquishness. The occasional reputation-destroying indiscretion.

Others immediately fill you with joyful anticipation. This feeling can be short-lived. Since there are only a few Fridays and Saturdays in this densely packed social season, you can almost bet you'll end up double- or triple-booked on that date. And even if you've mastered the art of flitting from one party to another without seeming rude, throw in a December storm and your ambitious schedule gets buried in snow, slush, and the vagaries of taxi service.

So much for being a guest. What if you're the host? Who do you invite? Whose noses will be out of joint if they're not invited? What if a mutual friend (with many of the same mutual friends) has a party on one of those heavily subscribed Fridays or Saturdays?

'Tis the season to be merry? How about the season to be anxious? As a customer facing some related conflicts in December once remarked to me, *There's nothing like Christmas to suck the joy right out of you.*

But let's push back against the stress associated with being a guest or a host. Assuming that you will (a) be invited to at least one potluck, and/or (b) have people drop in over the next few weeks, here are a few recipes that—provided you have the right spices—will make your life much less anxious. They are simple, unpretentious, and tasty, and what's even better: they're quick to prepare and delicious to enjoy any time of the year.

Smoky Oaxacan Shrimp

Pasilla de Oaxaca Flakes, Basil or Coriander

SERVES 4

The ingredient that gives these shrimp their Mexican flair is the pasilla, a chili that has taken a long journey to get to your kitchen. It is grown in the high Sierra Mije (*MEE-eh*) in the state of Oaxaca (*wha-HA-ka*) by the Mixtec people. The dark red chilies are left to dry on the plant until nearly black. Then they are picked, dried some more, and smoked in a traditional adobe. They are carried on horseback down the mountains and picked up at roadside for their trip to markets in Puebla and Oaxaca every December. So as rare as they are, the pasillas can be considered appropriate for a seasonal treat.

The flaking takes place at the Spice Trekkers facility in Montréal, and creates the most convenient form of these fruity, smoky, moderately hot chilies for everyday use.

4 tablespoons olive oil
Pasilla de Oaxaca Flakes to taste
3 garlic cloves, chopped
1 pound medium raw shrimp, peeled
salt to taste
juice of 1 lime
chopped fresh basil *or* coriander to taste

1. In a wok, heat the olive oil, Pasilla de Oaxaca Flakes, and garlic on high.
2. Once oil is well-infused, add shrimp and stir-fry, 2–3 minutes.
3. Season with salt and lime juice in final stages of cooking.
4. Garnish with basil (or coriander).

Warm Za'atar Olives

Za'atar

SERVES 6

Za'atar is one of the classic Middle Eastern blends and a versatile friend in the kitchen. It takes its name from za'atar thyme—a seed containing thymol, the same ingredient that gives the more common Mediterranean herb—thyme—its taste, and which has antimicrobial and antibacterial properties. The blend also contains sesame seeds, sumac (a culinary form), sea salt, anise, fennel, cumin, and oregano. You can use Za'atar on grilled fish or poultry, or sprinkle it on warm flatbread that's been brushed with olive oil.

1 cup Moroccan olives *or* other brineless olives
2 tablespoons olive oil
2 teaspoons Za'atar
Optional: half of 1 preserved lemon, seeded and cut into thin strips

1. Place a small frying pan on low heat. Add Moroccan olives and olive oil.
2. Stir occasionally until hot, about 5 minutes. Add strips of preserved lemon, if you choose. Sprinkle Za'atar and stir gently for 30 seconds.
3. Serve olives warm or at room temperature.

30

Over and Over and Over

Repetition has a bad reputation.

Repetitive work. Rote learning. Repetitive Stress Injury. Who has a kind word to say for any of them? *Groundhog Day* caught my attention when it came out in 1993 because it touched on one of my least favourite forms of repetition: anniversary shows in the news media. Catastrophes (Westray Mining Disaster, Swissair 111, 9/11), Christmas, big storms (from Hurricane Juan to the Groundhog Day gale of 1976)—you name it. It's like you've been driving along, taking in new and interesting sights, and suddenly notice there's a bull moose ahead, blocking the road. You check the date. Right. It's there every year on this day. No matter how many times you've encountered it in the past, there's no getting around it.

Years ago, I remember an older CBC announcer of Scottish extraction just months away from retirement telling me that he had got down on his knees in a story meeting to beg a young producer not to make him do the annual "Explain Hanukkah for us" interview. *I've been doing this for thirty-five years!* he pleaded. *I know more about Hanukkah than most Jews! Our audience will think I can't retain information for a year!*

But just as *Groundhog Day* was about much more than repetition (the writer James Parker calls it "a profound work of contemporary metaphysics") repetition is about much more than just doing something over and over again.

The French language recognizes this. *Une répétition* can be used the same way I've been using the word "repetition" so far. However, it can also be used in the sense of a rehearsal or practice, as when a ballerina dances a movement repeatedly for weeks or a basketball player spends hours taking hundreds of foul shots after his team has left the gym. It is the only way to perfect something. There are no shortcuts.

This kind of repetition is a hard sell in the age of trending Twitter topics. Extracting yourself from the constant flow of information and distractions is virtually impossible. I don't know how many future musicians we may have lost because Nintendo's Wii Rock Band Guitar appeared on the market in their tender years, creating the illusion that by playing a game they were learning how to play an instrument. Give them an actual guitar and they quickly hit a wall, which can only be scaled through practice. Never mind. There's a new edition of Wii with a different-shaped guitar. And when they tire of that, there will be no residue of learning.

People who perform repetition in the sense of rehearsing or practising must feel it's a topic they should avoid around people who don't. How do you begin to explain to your friends that you can't go clubbing because you have to be rested for a 6 A.M. training session? What young person wants to open a discussion of "sacrifice for long-term gain versus self-indulgence for instant gratification" with his or her peers? And, as you age, how do you find the boundary between repetition and routine?

Lately it has occurred to me that my father, who did all the cooking at his lunch counter, may have only known a handful of daily special dinner recipes. Roast Turkey, Baked Ham, Roast Beef, Boiled Salmon, Baked Pork Chops, Roast Pork, and Baked Halibut are the only ones I can recall. But he cooked them perfectly, repeating them for decades (with the fish on Fridays). He also knew the geography of his oil-fired stovetop like a guide knows the thickest woods—just *here* to simmer the potatoes so they wouldn't turn mushy before noon, and just *there* to pan-fry a hamburger without drying it out or burning it. When cooking, he was always in some zone between repetition and routine, working with complete efficiency because he'd done it so often.

There was satisfaction and confidence that came from that repetition, and I think that applies to the types of repetition I've mentioned. But can you use the experience that comes from doing something thousands of times to combat the "sameness" of the act?

At some point, when I was still working in broadcast journalism, I realized I had to convince myself that if I was going to fight the sense of dread about "anniversary shows" (*It's ECMA Weekend again! /As we approach this Remembrance Day…*), I would have to take them as a creative challenge. Yes, you might think you'd done every possible variation on a theme, but all you needed was one more variation for that year. And when you executed it well—thanks to accumulated experience and knowledge from all the times you'd explored the area before—it felt good, especially if a listener told you *I'd never heard that before* or *I'd never thought of it that way before.*

I don't know if this is going to rehabilitate the reputation of repetition. But maybe it will—if you read this book ten thousand times.

Roasted Pork Tenderloin

Cinnamon, Star Anise, Allspice, Peppercorn, Coriander, Mustard, Thyme

SERVES 4

I've always valued pork tenderloin because it's a quick cut of meat to roast and easy to slice into medallions. But after several decades of alternating between those two methods, I found that brining and spicing opened up many new taste possibilities.

Bryan Lowder writes the column "You're Doing it Wrong" for *Slate* magazine's culture blog, Browbeat. He believes pork tenderloin is what Julia Child would call a "wonder" of a hunk of protein. Giving meat an overnight soak in brine (salt and water) enhances its flavour and boosts its juiciness. The spice additions to the brine make this a truly special dish. Slice any leftovers for sandwiches.

1 cup Stutz or Tideview hard apple cider
3 tablespoons kosher salt
2 cups warm water
3 tablespoons brown sugar
1 stick cinnamon
1 star anise pod *or* ½ teaspoon anise or fennel
½ teaspoon allspice berries
½ teaspoon peppercorns
½ teaspoon coriander seeds
½ teaspoon mustard seeds
1 large bay leaf
3 sprigs fresh thyme
1 (1 pound) pork tenderloin
2 tablespoons olive oil

1 Combine hard cider, kosher salt, and brown sugar in a medium-sized bowl with warm water. Whisk to dissolve salt and sugar.

2 Gently crush cinnamon stick, star anise pod, allspice berries, peppercorns, coriander and mustard seeds with mortar and pestle. Combine spice and brine mixtures. Add thyme and bay leaf; stir gently.

3 Submerge pork tenderloin in brine, cover bowl with plastic wrap, and refrigerate at least 8 hours—preferably overnight.

4 Heat oven to 400°F (200°C). Remove tenderloin from brine, discard spice shards, and pat dry. Allow to return to room temperature, about 15 minutes. Line rimmed baking sheet with parchment paper.

5 Add olive oil to a large skillet on medium-high heat. When oil is hot, cook pork tenderloin, turning every 3–5 minutes, until browned all over, about 15 minutes.

6 Transfer tenderloin to baking sheet. Roast until juices run clear (meat thermometer 140°F [60°C]), 15–20 minutes.

7 Remove tenderloin from oven, cover loosely with foil, let rest 10 minutes and serve with roasted potatoes, sautéed apples, and caramelized onions.

star anise

Lobster Roll with East Coast Seafood Spices

East Coast Seafood Spice Blend

MAKES 4 ROLLS

Some seasonal favourites fall out of personal favour because, well, they've become too repetitive. The same old ingredients presented in the same old way, every year.

But whether it's a seaside picnic or in the backyard, there are few things that say "summertime" as eloquently as a lobster roll. Think about it: the sweet meat of the lobster, the citric tang of lemon or lime, the silky "mouth feel" of mayonnaise, and the crisp crunch of celery, scallions, and lettuce. Obviously, they need only one thing to complete this flavour bomb: spices.

It took Philippe and Ethné de Vienne eighteen months to develop their East Coast Seafood Spices Blend. Its composition was critiqued by their staff over many noon meals in the Spice Trekkers' Montréal atelier. (Why didn't I ever work at a place where the boss cooked lunch every day?) The final list includes celery seeds, pepper, chili, ginger, mustard, paprika, bay leaves, cloves, allspice, mace, green cardamom, and cassia.

Lobster Roll

4 rolls (hot dog, kaiser, *or* ciabatta)
4 teaspoons butter
shredded lettuce

Lobster Salad

3 cups cooked, diced lobster meat
3 tablespoons mayonnaise
1 tablespoon lemon *or* lime juice
2 scallions, thinly sliced
½ cup finely chopped celery
2 teaspoons East Coast Seafood Spice Blend, ground
salt and pepper to taste

1. Butter butter outside or inside of each roll (outside for hot dog rolls; inside for kaiser and ciabatta)" Toast each buttered side 2 minutes on a hot pan; meanwhile, mix salad ingredients in a bowl.
2. Place some lettuce in each hot roll.
3. Add lobster salad.
4. Sprinkle spices on top. Serve.

East Coast Crab Cakes

East Coast Seafood Spice Blend

MAKES 6 CRAB CAKES

Nobody has ever been arrested for drinking red wine with haddock, or white wine with roast beef. Likewise, when it comes to spices, there are no regulations about which dishes you're allowed to season with what. When you scanned the list of ingredients in East Coast Seafood Spices, I'll bet some of you imagined them seasoning any number of vegetable or poultry dishes. But there's no doubt these spices have a special affinity for seafood, like these East Coast Crab Cakes.

2 slices bread
1 small glass milk
1 egg
2 tablespoons mayonnaise
1 teaspoon Worcestershire sauce
2 teaspoons Dijon mustard
3 scallions, finely chopped
½ tablespoon East Coast Seafood Spice Blend, ground
1 pound crab meat, cleaned
4 tablespoons vegetable oil

1. Remove the bread crust and cut the slices into cubes. Place in a bowl and barely cover with milk. Let rest 1 minute, then using your hands squeeze out the excess milk. Throw out the milk and keep the bread.
2. Place the bread in a bowl with the egg, mayonnaise, Worcestershire, mustard, scallions, and spices. Knead well.
3. Add the crab and mix with a fork. Make 6 crab cakes with your hands.
4. Heat a pan on medium heat. Pour the oil and brown the crab cakes for 3 minutes on either side. Serve with lemon wedges.

Acknowledgements

My string of good fortune began by being born in Canada.

My mother and father enriched my life in countless ways that can't be found in parenting books. Between my childhood home and Nick's Coffee Counter—the family business—they gave me the love, limits, and opportunities required to grow as a human being. They let me serve customers from an early age, which introduced me to a colourful pageant of humanity and the arithmetic of making change. They didn't supervise my reading of comics, magazines, newspapers, tabloids, and paperbacks that came into the store, which whetted a lifelong appetite for unfiltered general knowledge. They let me create banana splits. It took a long time for me to appreciate how much of an educational advantage all of that afforded me. Nicholas Halavrezos and Hilda Mary Bohan—I thank you, love you, and miss you.

If I have any good qualities as a writer, most of the credit goes to the high expectations of the fine teachers at St. Malachy's Memorial High School in Saint John, New Brunswick.

Talk is cheap, but a well-crafted intro is pure gold. For decades, my colleagues at CBC Radio provided the editorial process that kept me from ever becoming intellectually lazy about what I wrote. They also granted me total freedom to pursue interesting topics to share with listeners, every day. To those colleagues and to all citizens who support public broadcasting whether they like it or not, thank you.

I wish to thank Philippe and Ethné de Vienne of Spice Trekkers/Épices de Cru in Montréal for proving that fairness, enthusiasm, hunches, and a handshake can form the foundation of a good business relationship.

To the Nimbus crew of Patrick Murphy and my editor Whitney Moran (she of the laser vision for at least seven types of ambiguity and the occasional missing ingredient): you've invented painless publishing.

My hasty transformation into a spice merchant was facilitated by neighbourhood friends in Dartmouth. Credits to the graphic skills of Greg Simon, the scientific recipe-vetting and test-kitchen of Guy Boulanger, the spiced creations of Mike Wood, the collaboration of Darrell MacDonald, Don Cormier, and Carol Short in ensuring that I receive my spice deliveries, and the always timely hospitality of Deb Woolway and Allee Andrews. Above all, I must thank Ruth Rintoul for her wisdom, good cheer, and more organizational support than anyone in my position could dare to expect.

To my sister Georgia and her son Anthony, thank you for remaining close even when you're hours away.

Finally, a brief elaboration of the dedication to this collection. Thanks to my eldest son, Nick, who turned me into an adult when he was born, awes me with his cooking skills and determination, and who set my course on the Spice Route. Together with Al and Maria, these three adult children allow me to lead an exciting life, vicariously, through their accomplishments. They also have an uncanny ability—individually and as a pack—to target parental foibles for deft shots. *Nai!*

And for Jennifer, who already works too hard, this just in: "Loading and unloading boxes of spice at 6 A.M. and 1 P.M. on your day off" was not in the marriage vows. But thank you for that and everything else you do, which is more than I deserve. All my love. You make my life of good fortune complete.

Bibliography

Alexander, Christopher, et al. *A Pattern Language: Towns, Buildings, Construction*. New York: Oxford University Press, 1977.

Beaulieu, Mirelle. *The Cooking of Provincial Quebec*. Toronto: Gage Toronto, 1975.

Gill, Janice Murray. *The Great Canadian Bread Book*. Scarborough: McGraw-Hill Ryerson, 1993.

Hemphill, Ian and Kate. *The Spice and Herb Bible*. Toronto: Robert Rose, 2006.

Keay, John. *The Spice Route: A History*. Berkeley: University of California Press, 2006.

Lehrer, Jonah. *Proust Was A Neuroscientist*. Boston: Houghton Mifflin Harcourt, 2007.

McPhee, John. *The Founding Fish*. New York: Farrar, Strous and Giroux, 2003.

Milton, Giles. *Nathaniel's Nutmeg: Or the True and Incredible Adventures of the Spice Trader Who Changed the Course of History*. New York: Penguin, 2000.

Proust, Marcel. *Remembrance of Things Past. Volume 1: Swann's Way: Within a Budding Grove*. Translated by C. K. Scott Moncrieff and Terence Kilmartin. New York: Vintage, 1982.

Recipe Credits

Courtesy of Allrecipes.com

Roasted Tomato Salsa (p. 32) recipe submitted by "Katkro"

Bread Pudding with Lebanese Seven Spice (p. 41) recipe submitted by "Ellenmarie"

Spiced Quinoa (via Ann MacDonald) (p. 87) recipe submitted by "Cinderella"

Linda Lee Oland and Guy Boulanger, inspired by *Elegant and Inspired: Vij's Indian Cuisine* (Douglas and McIntyre, 2006) by Vikram Vij and Meeru Dhalwalla

Cardamom Rice Pudding (p. 64)

Courtesy of Guy Boulanger

Gingerbread Loaf (p. 20)

Mexican-style Grilled Corn (p. 105)

Jambalaya (p. 130)

Courtesy of Guy Boulanger and Spicetrekkers.com

Jerk Chicken (p. 110)

Courtesy of J. Bryan Lowder, originally published on Browbeat (*Slate* magazine's culture blog): slate.com/blogs/browbeat

Roasted Pork Tenderloin (p. 158)

Adapted from *The Cotton Country Collection* (1972), courtesy of the Junior League of Monroe, LA
Broiled Peppercorn Shrimp (p. 143)

Courtesy of Louise Renault, adapted from *The French Farmhouse Cookbook* by Susan Herrmann Loomis (Workman Publishing Co., 1996)
Clafoutis (p. 10)

Courtesy of Manon Lapalme of Les Saveurs Unies, Terrebonne, Québec
Chai Shortbread (p. 60)

Courtesy of Michael Wood
Spicy Cheese Bites (p. 85)

Courtesy of Jean-Georges Vongerichten
Bloody Paradise (p. 92)

Courtesy of Nicole Ata, from the Patissier Bernd Siefert, as published in *Gourmet* magazine
Cassia Bud Cookies (p. 61)

Courtesy of Rachel Pitts, The Hungry Girls: hungrygirls.com.au
Sweet Potato, Green Bean, and Smoked Paprika Salad (p. 149)

Courtesy of Chef Renée Lavallée: Feistychef.ca
Renée's Chorizo and Okra Gumbo (p. 126)

Courtesy of Ruth Rintoul and Spicetrekkers.com
Information on Vanilla Pods (p. 8)
Information on Sweet Smoked Spanish Paprika (p. 147)

The Spice and Herb Bible **by Ian and Kate Hemphill (Robert Rose Inc., 2006)**
Lamb Shanks Tajine (p. 51)

Courtesy of Spicetrekkers.com
Lemon Vanilla Syrup (p. 11)
Leek, Yoghurt, and Mint Soup (p. 46)
Berberé Roast Chicken (p. 69)
Mesta Village Pasta (p. 72)
Warm Goat Cheese and Tomato Meze (p. 76)
Spiced Mayonnaise (p. 86)
Thousand-and-One-Nights Chicken (p. 97)
Country-style Lentil Soup with Panch Phoran (p. 114)
Peppercorn Chicken (p. 121)
Smoky Oaxacan Shrimp (p. 153)

New Greek Cuisine: Fresh and Modern Recipes from Aristedes' Kitchen**, co-authored by Chef Aristedes Pasparakis and Byron Ayanoglu (HarperCollins, 2005)**
Ageopelagiotiki Astakomakaronatha (Aegean Islands-style Lobster Pasta) (p. 134)

Adapted from *New Recipes From Moosewood Restaurant* (Moosewood Collective, 1987) courtesy of Salty's Restaurant, Halifax
West African Peanut and Sweet Potato Stew (p. 93)

Courtesy of *Vegetarian Times* magazine, via Gwen Houstoun
Caribbean Black Beans and Cornbread (p. 28)